A WORD ABOUT LANGUAGE

In the 17th and 18th centuries there were no common standards for spelling (even for names), punctuation, or capitalization. Writers spelled words as they sounded and capitalized words *within* sentences. In many instances, this book preserves the original spellings.

Women of Colonial America

Other Books in the Women of Action Series

Women of Colonial America

13 STORIES OF COURAGE AND
SURVIVAL IN THE NEW WORLD

Brandon Marie Miller

CHICAGO
REVIEW
PRESS

Parts of this book were originally published as *Good Women of a Well-Blessed Land, Women's Lives in Colonial America* (Minneapolis, MN: Lerner Publishing, 2003). It has been substantially revised, updated, and expanded.

Library of Congress Cataloging-in-Publication Data
Names: Miller, Brandon Marie.
Title: Women of Colonial America : 13 stories of courage and survival in the New World / Brandon Marie Miller.
Description: First edition. | Chicago, Illinois : Chicago Review Press, 2016. | Series: Women of action | "Parts of this book were originally published as Good Women of a Well-Blessed Land, Women's Lives in Colonial America (Minneapolis, MN: Lerner Publishing, 2003). It has been substantially revised, updated, and expanded"—Title page verso. | Includes bibliographical references and index.
Identifiers: LCCN 2015028517 | ISBN 9781556524875 (hardback)
Subjects: LCSH: Women—United States—Biography—Juvenile literature. | Women—United States—History—17th century—Juvenile literature. | Women—United States—History—18th century—Juvenile literature. | United States—History—Colonial period, ca. 1600–1775—Biography—Juvenile literature. | United States—Social life and customs—To 1775—Juvenile literature. | BISAC: JUVENILE NONFICTION / History / United States / Colonial & Revolutionary Periods. | JUVENILE NONFICTION / Biography & Autobiography / Women.
Classification: LCC HQ1416 .M555 2016 | DDC 305.4097309/032—dc23
LC record available at http://lccn.loc.gov/2015028517

Interior design: Sarah Olson

CONTENTS

This book is for Anna and Audrey, with love.

Dedicated also to the women of Colonial America.
How I wish you'd left more of yourselves behind,
your stories in your own words.

ACKNOWLEDGMENTS

MANY THANKS TO the wonderful people at museums, libraries, historical societies, and historic sites who helped with photo research for this book. A special thanks to staff at Colonial Williamsburg—Marianne Martin, Visual Resources Librarian; Allison Heinbaugh, Reference Librarian at the John D. Rockefeller Library; and Hope Evans at the Randolph House for sharing her insight into Eve and others. Many thanks to Cricket and Viv who went on an adventure to find Sarah Kemble Knight. Also, a special thanks to Mary Rose Quinn at the Stevens Memorial Library in North Andover, Massachusetts, who granted permission to use an image of Anne Bradstreet's work written in Anne's own hand. "We are just so pleased," she wrote, "to give more people access and spread the word about Anne Bradstreet in this way. Can't wait to read your book." Sweet music to my ears!

—BRANDON MARIE MILLER
www.brandonmariemiller.com

Women of Colonial America

I

The Natural Inhabitants

*"We were entertained with all love, and kindness, and
with as much bounty . . . as they could possibly devise."*
—Englishman Arthur Barlowe, writing of
his welcome by Native Americans, 1584

THE SUN WAS JUST slipping below the treetops when word spread
that a rowboat ferrying two white men approached the Roanoke
village. The wife of the chief's brother hastened to the water's
edge to greet the strangers. She gave a few quick orders and her
people dragged the strangers' boat onto the sand and carried the
two white men ashore on their backs. The woman escorted the
men to her home, a five-room lodge built from sweet-smelling
cedar.

Inside, she offered her guests seats by the fire. Her servants
dried the strangers' wet clothes and bathed their feet in warmed
water. She presented dish after dish for the strangers' pleasure:
venison stew, boiled fish, juicy melons, wine, and water flavored
with sassafras, ginger, and black cinnamon.

Suddenly, several men entered the house carrying bows and arrows. Fear froze the strangers' faces, and the woman asked the hunters to leave their weapons outside. At the evening's end, her guests rowed back to their ship, laden with gifts of food and invitations to return.

The two guests were English explorers under the patronage of Sir Walter Raleigh. In the written report of their visit to present-day North Carolina, the gracious Native American woman is referred to only as "the wife of Granganimo the king's brother." But the Englishmen praised her beauty, admired her coral and pearl jewelry, and commented on the fine copper earrings worn by her servants. They also heaped praise upon the villagers, "for a more kinde and loving people there can not be found in the worlde."

Like many Native American women before and after her, Granganimo's wife greeted Europeans with generosity and aid. And like many native women before and after her, the reward she received for her hospitality was one of pain. Not many years later, the first English colonists at Roanoke burned her village to the ground.

HOUSEHOLD AFFAIRS

In 1600 an estimated 400,000 Native Americans lived in the lands east of the Appalachian Mountains, farming, hunting, and fishing along a coast that stretched from Canada down to Florida. They were diverse peoples who spoke different languages, followed different customs, and worshipped in different ways.

Most Native Americans lived in villages, some a small collection of dwellings, others in large communities of 50 lodges or more surrounded by a stockade of sharpened logs. Within the larger group of the tribe, people banded together by family ties into clans. Villagers hiked networks of trails through towering primeval forests. They canoed rivers far and wide to trade and build alliances for war and peace among other tribes.

Native American town of Pomeiock, Theodore de Bry, engraver, 1590.
Library of Congress, LC-USZ62-54018

War, trade, and hunting often summoned men away for weeks at a time, but a woman's life revolved around the village and home. "In the management of household affairs the husband leaves everything to his wife and never interferes," explained missionary David Zeisberger, who lived among the

Lenni Lenape (the Delaware). Her hard work fed and clothed and sheltered the tribe.

Daily, a woman fetched water and gathered wood to stoke her cooking fires and warm the home. She created the tools she needed and the goods her family used—she wove baskets, made clay pots, sewed leather pouches, and fashioned dishes out of tree bark.

Women also built the family home. Among tribes like the Wampanoag, Narragansett, and Powhatan, women wove mats from dried grasses and cattails, often weaving designs into their work. In the late 1630s, English colonist Roger Williams noted that Narragansett homes were "embroydered" so beautifully that the designs made "as fair a show as Hangings [tapestries] with us." Mat by mat, a woman layered her handiwork over an arching framework of poles. The one-room houses measured about 16 feet long and 14 feet across with a smoke hole in the roof covered by a flap. In hot weather she rolled up the sides of her house to catch cooling breezes. And her house was

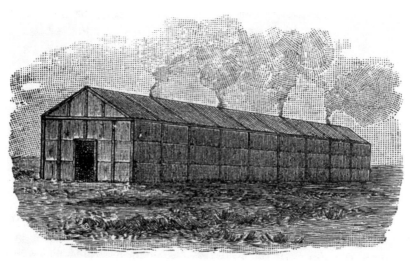

Iroquois longhouse.
US History Images

portable—she could pack poles and mats for a quick move to winter hunting grounds or summer planting fields.

Iroquois women covered their great longhouses with bark. Some of these houses measured 50 to 100 feet long and housed up to 20 families. Women in southern tribes, like the Cherokee and the Choctaw, covered a rectangular frame of poles with a mixture of packed clay and crushed shells, bark, or grasses under a snug thatched roof.

"SHE COOKS VICTUALS REGULARLY"

Men provided meat and fish, but women provided all other foods. Unlike in Europe, where farm labor typically fell to men, women farmed in Native American villages. Just after dawn women headed to the fields with young children in tow. They worked together, singing and chatting, digging and hoeing with clamshells and deer-bone tools. Older women and children protected the crops from animals and birds, and one European settler observed women scolding wayward horses away from tender plants and fretting "at the very shadow of a crow."

Corn, beans, and squash—called the Three Sisters by the Iroquois—proved the main staples of Native American diets. Women planted several types of corn. James Adair, a trader in the Carolinas among the Cherokee, Catawba, and other tribes, described yellow "hommony corn," "small corn" that ripened quickly, and a large white corn called bread corn. Women spent hours grinding dried corn between two stones, turning out coarse whole-grain flour they mixed with water, patted into flat cakes, and baked nestled in hot ashes.

Besides the vegetables they grew, Native American women also picked wild fruits such as strawberries and cranberries. They dug edible roots and tubers in the forest, gathered baskets of nuts, and harvested clams along the shoreline. In late winter they collected sap from maple trees and boiled it into sweet syrup.

Native American women planting, Theodore de Bry, engraver, 1591.
Library of Congress, LC-USZ62-31869

Stews of meat, roots, and vegetables simmered over fires. Hunks of fresh meat roasted on spits, layers of dripping fat hissing into the flames. But much of a woman's food work involved drying and preserving food, work she did with sun and fire smoke. Survival depended upon dried corn stashed in large pots and buried in the ground, or the berries and thin strips of pumpkin, fish, and meats she'd carefully hung on racks to dry for the lean winter months.

Native American women controlled that most important of supplies—food. They decided how much and when food was doled out. If women wished to stop their men from going to war, they withheld the dried corn and dried meat needed to feed the war party. David Zeisberger marveled that once a man returned from the hunt he gave up all control over the meat. A woman "may then do what she pleases with it. [Her husband] says nothing, if she even gives the greatest part of it to her friends, which is a very common custom." Women did give generously; in providing for others "when meat has been secured" she earned the respect of her people.

CLOTHES ON OUR BACKS

Animals provided hides for clothing as well as meat. Women soaked a hide in water and scraped off the hair. A second soaking in a chemical mixture of crushed deer brain and water further softened the hide. Next, a woman stretched the skin on a rack and rubbed it repeatedly with a stone, dull hatchet, or shell to force out the water and grease.

Once rubbed and dried, she had supple, pale leather ready to cut with a knife and sew into clothes using a bone needle and deer sinew (tendon) for thread. Skirts, shirts, leggings, and moccasins made from tanned skins felt buttery soft to the skin but easily withstood a harsh outdoor life. For winter warmth, Native American women fashioned thick fur robes and blankets. Women expressed their creative sides by decorating clothes and other objects with shells, bone beads, dyed porcupine quills, and paints.

"DOING JUST WHAT THEY LIKE"

Native American women labored at physically demanding jobs. But they set their own work pace and usually shared the burden of chores. They also saved time for fun. In the 1630s, French missionary Gabriel Sagard grumbled that native women found "plenty of time to waste." Women enjoyed themselves "in gaming, going to dances and feasts, chatting and killing time," he wrote. Even worse, complained Sagard, the women were used to "doing just what they like with their leisure."

Many Native American women kept house with a single spouse. In some tribes a husband lived with more than one wife. A man might be expected to marry his brother's widow as a way of providing care for her. Some tribes believed a man should marry all the sisters in one family. The first or eldest wife usually held an honored status. The more wives, the more workers a household shared.

A would-be husband wooed his sweetheart—and her family —with gifts and sought permission from the bride's parents or an older female relative to court the girl. Often the man had to prove his worth. Could he provide meat and protection for a new wife? Some tribes subjected prospective grooms to a year-long test, observing him and his intended as the two lived with her family. In tribes of the Iroquois confederacy—the Cayuga, Mohawk, Oneida, Onondaga, and Seneca—the husband joined his wife's clan.

Either partner might freely end an unhappy union. The choice of walking away gave Native American women an independence not shared by white women. Yet the ease of dissolving a marriage did not make divorce common. "I know many couples," reported colonist Roger Williams, "that have lived twenty, thirty, forty yeares together." Rarely did one spouse put the other aside if they had children, who remained in the care of the mother and her clan. "The mother's title rests on the law of nature," noted Antoine de la Mothe, Sieur de Cadillac in the 1690s, "since no one can dispute that she is the mother of the children whom she had brought into the world."

MOTHERHOOD

Most native peoples believed pregnancy linked a woman to mysterious and dangerous forces of nature. "Pregnant women among them cause, they say, many misfortunes," reported Jesuit priest François du Peron, "for they cause the husband not to take anything in the hunt; if one of them enters a cabin where there is a sick person, he grows worse; if she looks at the animal that is being pursued, it can no longer be captured."

When she went into labor, a native woman left her home for a specially prepared hut. A midwife or relative might assist her, but she might also give birth on her own. As a warrior tested his bravery in battle, a woman displayed hers by not crying out through the pains of childbirth; surrendering to pain brought shame. An astounded Roger Williams observed that native women "are scarcely heard to groane" during childbirth. Not realizing native women were simply being brave, European males concluded native females must be formed differently than white women. "The [native] Women of America have very easy Travail [labor] with their children," noted southern trader John Lawson. "Besides, they are unacquainted with those severe Pains which follow the Birth in our European Women."

Native American mothers toted their infants upright in snug wooden cradle boards fashioned by the fathers. The mother decorated her child's cradle board with paint, beads, and feathers. Carrying the baby on her back freed her arms for work and, if needed, she propped the cradle board against a tree trunk or hung it from a branch. Mothers "diapered" their babies by stuffing moss or cattail fluff inside the cradle board around the child.

Early on, mothers taught their children to endure discomfort —dousing them with cold water or snow—to teach them survival skills. Mothers trained their daughters in the ways of women's work, encouraging even young girls to pound corn, gather sticks, and pull weeds. Native American mothers rarely struck their children, but relied on shame to mend bad behavior. Many Europeans, raised on the stern belief that beatings or whippings provided a good "correction," found this neglect of punishment shocking.

If a Native American mother wanted to scold her daughter, she might simply burst into tears and say, "Thou dishonourest me." Jesuit priest Pierre de Charlevoix declared, "It seldom happens that this sort of reproof [scolding] fails." The greatest punishment he witnessed was a mother flicking water in her child's face. "It would seem . . . that a childhood so ill instructed, should be followed by a very . . . turbulent state of youth," he wrote, "[but] the Indians are naturally quiet and . . . masters of themselves." Native American mothers set that example for their children from birth.

2

In This New Discovered Virginia

"In a newe plantation it is not knowen whether man or woman be the most necessary."

—*Virginia House of Burgesses, an elected legislature, July 1619*

IN MAY 1607, JUST over 100 Englishmen established a foothold along a wide river flowing into the Chesapeake Bay. They called their Virginia settlement "James Towne," named in honor of King James I. Most colonists considered themselves "gentlemen" and believed "Rooting in the ground" beneath their dignity— even if it meant growing the crops they needed to eat. They'd signed on for adventure and profit, expecting a quick return to a comfortable life in England. But grim realities soon set in. "Our men," wrote George Percy, "were destroyed with cruell diseases . . . but for the most part they died of mere famine. There was

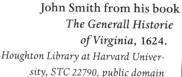

John Smith from his book
*The Generall Historie
of Virginia,* 1624.
*Houghton Library at Harvard Univer-
sity, STC 22790, public domain*

never Englishmen left in a for-
reigne Countrey in such miserie
as wee were in this new discovered
Virginia."

Less than a year and a half later, Captain John Smith recorded
the intrusion of English women into this struggling male world:
"The first gentlewoman and woman-servant . . . arrived." The
new arrivals were Mistress Forrest, wife of a colonist, and her
teenage maid, Anne Burras. As a single female, 15-year-old
Anne's status soared from simple servant to great prize. Within
two months she married John Laydon, a carpenter, in the colony's first wedding.

The raw condition of their new home most likely shocked
the two women. Crowded huts with dirt floors served as houses.
Such heat and sweltering humidity they'd seldom experienced
in England. Didn't heat sap fluid from a person's blood? "Great
Sweating," warned medical writer William Vaughan, left the
"inner parts" cold and withered. Colonists fell ill with "ague"
(probably malaria) and suffered through waves of chills and
fevers, nausea and vomiting.

This new land, though beautiful, seemed wild and savage,
infested with insects and vermin. Unable to raise enough crops,
the colonists relied mostly on corn supplied by Native Americans
and the dwindling foodstuffs brought on their ships. Mistress

Forrest, around 35 years old, died the same year she arrived, her remains buried within the fort at Jamestown.

In August 1609 Jamestown welcomed a new wave of colonists, swelling the population to about 500 souls, including more women and some children. But the dark days continued in Virginia. Colonists died of sickness, hunger, and skirmishes with the Native Americans. Starvation stalked the colony, aided by disease and a drought that worsened food and water issues. Tribal people suffered with the drought as well, and harvested fewer baskets of food for their own needs, let alone the ever-increasing demands of the colonists.

By the spring of 1610, only 60 men, women, and children had survived what became known as the starving time. They had gnawed acorns, roots, rats, snakes, horses, and dogs. John Smith reported one man murdered "his wife as she slept . . . , and fedd upon her till he had clean devoured all her parts save-inge [except] her head."

Many wondered if Smith exaggerated, but according to recent research, one of those consumed was a 14-year-old girl, her name lost to history, but called "Jane" by the archaeologists who discovered her remains. Jane had died of starvation or disease, and her bones tell a story of desperation: the girl's skull and a leg bone show clear butcher marks of knife and hatchet blades.

"THE WANT OF WIVES"

As early as 1609 broadsides posted in England urged single women to emigrate to Jamestown "for the better strengthening of the colony." Virginia offered men eager to wed, a new home, and a new life—if only a woman grasped this brass ring of adventure. The colony's need for women grew so desperate that kidnappers snatched females off English streets and sold them in Virginia as servants. One song lilting through London's taverns told the tale of "The Woman Outwitted: or the Weaver's Wife cunningly catch'd in a Trap, by her Husband, who sold her for ten Pounds, and sent her to Virginny."

In 1619, members of the Virginia Company, who hoped to reap large profits from America's resources, actively recruited "wives for Virginia." They recognized that a shipload of females would "tye and roote the Planters myndes [minds] to Virginia by the bonds of wives and children." About 90 women arrived in Virginia in February and March 1620.

A new campaign in 1621 sought "younge, handsome, and honestlie educated Maides." Young women hoping for selection supplied recommendations laced with words like *honest, sober,* and *industrious.* They listed skills sure to attract a man in the wilderness—besides their obvious feminine charms—claiming talents in brewing, baking, and sewing.

The Virginia Company picked 57 women "specially recommended for their good bringing up." The women ranged in age from 15 to 26. Most of them, like Martha Baker, were around 20 years old. Three of them, like Elizabeth Grinbey, age 26, were widows. Twenty women, like Jane Dier, were teenagers. Eleven of the women, including Lucy Remnant, had no parents, while 11 others, like Elizabeth Neville, had lost their fathers.

What courage or desperation drove a young woman to make the dangerous voyage across the Atlantic to an uncertain future? They must have prayed for a good husband from among the "honest and industrious Planters." They had no illusions about their place—they were women bought and paid for. The planters reimbursed the Virginia Company for the cost of bringing their future brides to the colony—150 pounds of Virginia's new currency, tobacco.

In addition to the promise of a husband, the Virginia Company supplied each woman with petticoats, caps, an apron, two pairs of shoes, and six pairs of sheets. Within months of their arrival in the autumn of 1621, many of the women had, indeed, married.

AN UNKNOWN WORLD

Newly arrived females must have wondered what this new world meant for them. In England, a woman could buy bread—or at least a sack of flour—from the baker or miller in the village. At home she might grow vegetables and herbs in a patch of kitchen garden. She might keep a cow or a few goats to milk, then churn the cream into cheese and butter. She could buy cloth to sew clothes. But in Jamestown, she found these simple acts difficult or impossible.

Society itself was missing—where were the farmers, laborers, and servants? Where were the craftsmen, tradespeople, and merchants with their wares? Where were the churchmen and the great stone cathedrals? Where were the lords and ladies, the gentlefolk, clad in laces and velvet and silk?

Most of all, where were the other women? Everywhere a Jamestown woman looked, she saw men, six men at least for every female face. She would never consider Virginia's other females—the Native American women—her equal. Indeed, the Jamestown colonists often huddled behind their stockade walls, fearful to venture into dark woods filled with "skulking savages."

Unlike Native Americans, colonists had little experience hunting game or searching for edible plants. There might be fish in the sea, birds in the air, and beasts in the forest, but as John Smith noted early on, "They are so wild and we so weake and ignorant, we cannot much trouble them [by hunting.]"

Chopping down enough trees to create farm fields seemed overwhelming. In England, where fields had long ago been cleared, most people didn't have to wield an ax for such work. How could they possibly hack down a thick forest to clear a field "penetrable For the Plough" wondered one colony investor. Until colonists adopted the slash-and-burn method used by the Native Americans, clearing a field remained an immense task.

FIRST CONTACT BETWEEN TWO WORLDS

Jamestown lay in an area inhabited by Algonquin-speaking tribes, unified under a powerful man the English called Powhatan. Even before the first colonists rowed ashore at Jamestown, people of the Powhatan Confederacy—as well as other Native Americans—had sampled European goods carried by traders and explorers to the New World.

The strangers with their pale skin and many shades of hair aroused curiosity in native people. European ships, so much larger than any native canoe, seemed like floating islands on the sea. And the white people wore clothes in colors and fabrics amazing to behold. Sunlight flashed from the men's helmets and armored breastplates. The women wore heavy, restricting clothing from chin to ankles.

Besides their appearance, the Europeans possessed wonders: iron hoes, mirrors, clocks, and books. Their copper kettles were so thin, yet unbreakable. The blades of their knives and hatchets gleamed sharper and stronger than anything the native people had. Most startling of all were the guns carried by the newcomers that exploded in smoke and noise louder than any crack of thunder. From first contact, Native Americans traded food and expertise for the amazing gifts of the Europeans.

English men and women held native culture and religion as inferior to their own. Even treatment of a tribe's women shocked the Europeans. To their eyes, native men forced women to do all the work while the men spent their time hunting and fishing—sporting fun to the English. The women's lives, wrote John Smith, "be very painful and the men often idel. The women and children do the rest of the work." Roger Williams, a colonist in New England, marveled, "It is almost incredible what burthens [burdens] the poore women carry of Corne, of Fish, of Beanes, of Mats, and a childe besides."

Contact with the English meant contact with European diseases that native people had never encountered before: smallpox,

Detail of Powhatan, from John Smith's Map of Virginia, 1612.
Library of Congress, LC-USZ62-73206

measles, diphtheria, plague, and influenza. Europeans regularly exposed to such illnesses had built up some resistance, but the Native Americans had no immunity. Raging fevers, vomiting, diarrhea, and racking coughs spread from lodge to lodge, leaving no one well enough to fetch water, food, or wood. In some cases, disease wiped out entire villages. Almost 90 percent of the Native Americans on the East Coast died of disease during the 1600s, that first century white colonists arrived to stay.

GROWING TENSIONS

The Powhatans and English colonists walked a tightrope between need, fear, and aggression, the relationship on both sides marked by skirmishes and hostage taking. In 1608 Powhatan sent his "most deare and wel-beloved daughter," Pocahontas, to Jamestown. She came with a delegation seeking the return of Powhatan hostages. Smith eventually freed the warriors to honor the girl's presence. Pocahontas played an important role as peacekeeper in Jamestown's story, and following her death in 1617, and Powhatan's death a year later, hope for peace in Virginia died, too.

Virginia's native peoples had wearied of years of loss and English arrogance. They'd found little to admire in the English, except their weapons and goods, and had witnessed the destruction of forests, wild game, crops and fields, villages, and homes. After 15 years the Native Americans knew these colonists meant to plant roots, spread across the land, and never leave.

The Powhatan Confederacy, now led by Powhatan's half brother Opechancanough, pushed back against the advance. In the early morning of March 22, 1622, natives attacked Virginia's scattered James River settlements. More than 350 colonists perished that day, including some of the hopeful young women who'd arrived as "wives for Virginia." Opechancanough meant to drive the English from Virginia's shores, but the attack resulted in English outrage and swift revenge.

As Europeans and Native Americans struggled with one another, a third culture arrived in Virginia in 1619: about 20 Africans brought on a Dutch vessel. A few years later, just

Landing of Negroes at Jamestown from a Dutch Man-of-War, 1619, painted by
illustrator Howard Pyle in 1917.
Library of Congress, LC-USZ62-5334

months after the March attack by the Powhatans, an African
woman known as Mary arrived at Jamestown. She came not to
be a bride but to be a laborer, an indentured servant on a James
River tobacco farm.

Only five of the farm's 55 workers, some possibly slaves,
had survived the March 22 attack. Out of those five Mary wed

Antonio, an African man. Once freed from their contracts as indentured servants, Mary and her husband took the names Mary and Anthony Johnson. They settled on a 250-acre farm on Virginia's Eastern Shore. Later the couple leased 300 acres in Maryland and named their farm Tonies Vinyard. In 1676 their grandson John purchased 44 acres and called his place Angola, perhaps as tribute to the homeland of Anthony and Mary Johnson.

From the beginning, hardship and death hovered over Virginia. Between 1607 and 1625 nearly 6,500 people immigrated to the colony. But a census from 1625 told the dire story—a population of only 1,025 souls. Sadly, only 35 of the nearly 150 "younge and handsome Maides" who'd undertaken the incredible journey into the dangers of the New World remained alive.

Pocahontas
A Life in Two Worlds

LIKE A TAPESTRY WOVEN from both fact and legend, the story of Pocahontas leaves us wondering what is true about the most famous Native American woman. We know nothing of her own thoughts, and those few words attributed to her come from the pens of Englishmen. She lived at a turning point, a moment when life changed forever for the native peoples of North America.

Born around 1595 or 1596 and named Amonute, she was the daughter of Wahunsonacock, also called Powhatan, paramount leader of an Algonquian tribe in Tidewater Virginia. Her mother's name is lost to history, one of Powhatan's many wives, married for pleasure or as a means to bind her tribe to Powhatan's growing confederacy. The baby girl also possessed a private name, Matoaka. But she is best known by her childhood nickname, Pocahontas, meaning something like "playful one" or "mischief."

Powhatan reigned over thousands of square miles and a thriving society of roughly 15,000 people. He had inherited six chiefdoms and added to his power, conquering other tribes or gathering them in through diplomacy and marriage alliances. Each tribe had their own subchief, or *werowance*, and paid yearly tributes to Powhatan in corn, tanned hides, Chesapeake pearls, and shell beads.

A wife lived in Powhatan's household until she bore a child, and then she withdrew to her own people. When the child reached age four or five mother and child returned to Powhatan, living and working beside a host of half siblings and step-mothers. Pocahontas was probably born at Powhatan's chief residence on the edge of the York River, the village of Werowocomoco. Pocahontas grew up as a favorite of her powerful father, his "dearest jewell" one colonist recorded. Like many girls and women in her village, she was strong and athletic, and also curious, funny, and outgoing. She sought attention in her father's crowded household—the "playful one" up to "mischief," Pocahontas. All children, even the daughters of Powhatan, worked for the survival of the family. Pocahontas would have tended crops, woven mats, gathered wood, and dug in the forests and stream shallows for food.

The arrival of English colonists in the spring of 1607 changed the course of Pocahontas's life along with the lives of all Native Americans in Virginia. She probably saw her first Englishman in late 1607, when Powhatan warriors captured Captain John Smith and marched him to Werowocomoco. Captain Smith looked different than anyone she'd ever seen—his hair, his skin, his clothes. How much contact they had is unknown, although Smith had his own tales to tell about the girl.

In later writings, John Smith described the central event in the legend of Pocahontas, set during his capture in December 1607. At first, Powhatan treated Smith well and "feasted him after their best barbarous manner." Suddenly warriors surrounded him, dragging him toward two great stones, where they stretched him flat and forced his head down. With war

An 1870 print shows a grown-up Pocahontas saving John Smith's life.
Library of Congress, LC-USZ62-17680

clubs raised over his head, Smith expected any second to have
his brains beaten out. Instead, Pocahontas rushed to his side and
pleaded for his life. When her words failed to move her father
the girl took John's head in her arms "and laid her owne upon
his to save him from death: whereat the Emperour was contented he should live."

Did the event happen as Captain Smith said? Why had he not
written of it before the 1620s? Powhatan liked Smith and wanted
an alliance with the English. He may have used some ceremony
to make John a *werowance* or leader of the English within the
Powhatan Confederacy. Was it a ritual ceremony, a mock execution and saving, performed by the Powhatans with Pocahontas
playing the role of savior? As a child, it is unlikely Pocahontas
would have played any part in such an event. Also telling, Smith
claimed other adventures in Turkey and France where lovely

young women saved his life. Perhaps he penned the Virginia story as another embellishment for his readers, who clamored for exotic tales of adventure. Whatever the truth, the story of Pocahontas saving the life of Captain John Smith served as the keystone in her own legend.

In the spring of 1608 Pocahontas appeared at Jamestown, the log stockade the colonists had built alongside the James River in 1607. Along with one of her father's top advisors, she arrived as an agent of goodwill sent by Powhatan to secure the release of several Native Americans held captive at Jamestown. "Powhatan understanding we detaine certaine Salvages, sent his Daughter, a child of tenne years old," wrote John Smith. He noted in a 1608 report that, "for feature, countenance, and proportion," Pocahontas "much exceedeth any of the rest of his people: but for wit and spirit," he recorded, the girl had no equal.

She may even have spoken some English and served as a translator. An English boy, Thomas Savage, had lived with the Powhatan for the purpose of learning their language and customs, and Pocahontas may have shared in this exchange of languages. The colonists turned their captives over to Pocahontas, "the Kings Daughter, in regard of her fathers kindnesse in sending her." John Smith asked her to tell her father the English had treated the prisoners well and sent her off with "such trifles as contented her [gifts]."

For the next several years, relations between the colonists at Jamestown and the Powhatan tribes remained mostly peaceful. Pocahontas often visited the fort, delivering messages from her father. She led trade delegations laden with furs and food the Powhatans exchanged for hatchets, beads, and trinkets carried from England. William Strachey, the first secretary of the colony, described Pocahontas as "a well featured, but wanton yong girl Powhatan's daughter, sometymes resorting to our fort, of the age then of eleven or twelve years." He noted she would, "get the boyes forth with her into the markett place, and make them wheele, falling on their hands, turning up their heeles upwards, whome she would followe and wheele so her self, naked as she was, all the fort over."

John Smith and Pocahontas talked on these visits. In 1612, though he was no longer in Virginia, John added a list of words in her language—a language lost today—to his book, *A Map of Virginia with a Description of the Country, The Commodities, People, Government and Religion.* He also included a few complete sentences, and one can imagine him writing down the native words as they sounded to him, spoken by Pocahontas. One translates: "I am verie hungrie, what shall I eate?" The other, *"Kehaten pokahontas tiaquagh ningh tanks manotyens neer mowchick rawrenock audowgh,"* means "Bid Pokahontas bring hither two little Baskets, and I will give her white beads to make her a chaine."

As relations between colonists and natives deteriorated, Pocahontas visited Jamestown less often. The two sides needed one another for trade. The natives wanted metal—hatchets, pots, tools, and weapons. The colonists relied on corn from the Native Americans, even in times of drought and poor crops when the tribes had little to share. The English often took what they wanted with threats and a show of sword and gun. Deadly skirmishes, stealing, and hostage taking marked the uneasy relations.

In January 1609 Captain Smith led a trade party to Werowocomoco. Negotiations with Powhatan broke down; the paramount chief wanted swords in exchange for corn, and the English refused. Powhatan chided Smith that he came not for trade but to invade and possess his country. Smith recorded Powhatan's words: "What can you get by war, when we can hide our provision and flie to the woodes, whereby you must famish?" Powhatan wanted Smith to come not with weapons but with friendship. Later, under pressure from the English, Powhatan would indeed "flie to the woodes" and leave the English without aid.

According to Smith's 1624 account, Pocahontas stole through the forest to the English camp and warned him that Powhatan meant to kill the colonists. In return for her service, Smith wished to give her "Such things as shee delighted in, . . . but with the teares running downe her cheekes, shee said shee durst not be seene to haue [have] any: for if *Powhatan* should know it, she were but dead, and so shee ranne away by her selfe as she came." John and his men escaped thanks to the girl.

But again, what is true? As a protected and well-supervised child, Pocahontas racing through the frozen night to warn the colonists seems unlikely. And the English, already on guard, suspicious, and armed to the teeth, would hardly have needed a warning that their lives were in danger. Maybe it happened, maybe not. But in October that year an explosion injured Smith so badly that he returned to England. When Pocahontas next came to the fort she was told he had died.

Pocahontas probably married around 1610 at the age of 12 or 13. William Strachey reported that Powhatan had 20 sons and 10 daughters, and "younge Pocohunta, a daughter of his, using soemtyme to our fort in tymes past, nowe married to a private captaine, called Kocoum, some two yeares since." To the English, a "private captaine" meant a warrior in Powhatan's personal guard. No one knows who Kocoum was or how he and Pocahontas met. Pocahontas was free to encourage or quash any suitor's wooing. To wed her, the groom would have paid Powhatan enough goods to compensate the chief for the loss of his daughter. There is no mention in any written record, but native oral history claims she had a child with Kocoum.

As Pocahontas began life as a married young woman, continued warfare marked English-Powhatan relations. The colonists established other settlements along the James River, spreading out from the original fort's safety. Both sides captured hostages. If John Smith's 1607 capture and rescue by Pocahontas is the most well-known part of her legend, a second kidnapping received much less notice—the kidnapping of Pocahontas by the English.

In the spring of 1613 Captain Samuel Argall began a trading journey to the Patawomeck tribe. Along the route he heard news that changed his plans: "I was told . . . that the Great Powhatan's daughter Pokahuntis was with the great King Patawomeck." Argall resolved to capture the girl, "by any stratagem that I could use." He saw Pocahontas as a most valuable hostage. The English could use her to force food from Powhatan and the return of English captives and stolen weapons.

Argall met with a subchief named Yapassus, also spelled Japazaws. "If he did not betray Pokohuntis unto my hands, wee would no longer be brothers nor friends," Argall threatened. When Yapassus protested that Powhatan would declare war against him, Argall replied if he did not help, the English would declare war. On the other hand, the English could defend him against Powhatan.

Pocahontas had been with the Patawomeck for about three months, probably acting as an envoy representing Powhatan. With assurances Pocahontas would not be hurt, Yapassus and his wife connived to get the girl on board Argall's ship. The wife pretended she wanted to visit the English ship and her husband would not allow it unless Pocahontas accompanied her. An Englishman later wrote, "Now was the greatest labor to win her," for Pocahontas may have been suspicious that all wasn't right. She relented, however, and boarded the ship, where Argall gave them a tour and dinner. Then he proposed the women rest in a private room while he conducted business with Yapassus.

When Pocahontas returned to the men, she said she wanted to go ashore. Instead, Argall told her, "she must goe with him, and compound peace betwixt her Countrie and us, before she ever should see *Powhatan*." Now, wrote Ralph Hamor, Pocahontas turned "pensive and discontented," and through "extraordinary curetous useage," little by little the English persuaded her to remain patient. She must have vented some of her frustration at Yapassus, for one Englishman recorded that the man repeatedly proclaimed his innocence in the whole affair. Argall sent a messenger to Powhatan demanding he release his English captives, return all stolen weapons and tools, and provide the colonists with corn. If not, Pocahontas would remain in English hands. The messenger returned with word that Powhatan felt deep grief at Pocahontas's situation and asked the English to treat her well. He would give them what they demanded in exchange for her. On April 13, with Pocahontas onboard, Argall sailed to Jamestown.

The earliest mention of her kidnapping was a brief summary from colonist Samuel Purchas in 1613: "They tooke Pokahuntis prisoner, and for her ransome had Corne, and redeliverie of their prisoners and weapons." The story of Yapassus's involvement in the kidnapping first appeared in the 1615 writings of Ralph Hamor. This account justified Argall's actions as a means to reclaim captured Englishmen, easy to do when Yapassus "would have betrayed his owne father" for a copper kettle and trinkets.

Samuel Argall and his captive arrived at the Jamestown stockade. John Smith, writing years later, noted Powhatan loved both his daughter and English goods. For three months the chief did nothing about his daughter's ransom. Then Powhatan, under pressure from the English, returned some of the captives and a mere portion of the goods the colonists wanted. He promised the rest, plus bushels of corn, when they delivered Pocahontas safely to freedom. But the English played hardball—Pocahontas would remain a prisoner until Powhatan met all their demands.

The English eventually removed her from the fort to a new settlement called Henrico, near present-day Richmond, where an enthusiastic young reverend, Alexander Whitaker, began her conversion to Christianity. He believed the Virginia natives needed only Christian enlightenment and education to turn into productive citizens of the English world. Their intellect and understanding, he wrote, was as great as any Englishman. He was not surprised at Pocahontas's quick intelligence as the young woman spent hours working on her English and studying the teachings of Christianity.

As a hostage, Pocahontas lived immersed in an alien world, dressed in the heavy, constricting clothes of an Englishwoman, her black hair hidden beneath a linen cap. She ate English foods like peas, onions, and cabbages while sitting at a table set with plates, cups, and knives and drank wine poured from glass bottles.

By July 1613 Pocahontas had met a tobacco planter named John Rolfe. He had sailed for Jamestown with his pregnant wife—her name unknown today—and faced hardship when their ship ran aground during a storm off Bermuda in 1610. Their baby girl died there, and John's wife died not long after they finally arrived at Jamestown. He had success growing Spanish tobacco in Virginia, the tobacco used by the natives proving too strong for European tastes. Rolfe's work with tobacco farming brought Virginia a cash crop that transformed the colony.

After Pocahontas had spent nearly a year in captivity, the Virginia governor, Sir Thomas Dale, took her onto a ship and, with a troop of nearly 150 armed men, sailed to Powhatan's lands. Dale meant to force payment of the remaining ransom. The natives attacked, their arrows flying among the English ships. The English rowed ashore, burned Native American homes, and destroyed everything they could find. Then they sailed farther up river.

Pocahontas met on board with two of her brothers. According to Sir Thomas she told the men she felt anger that her father had valued her less than old English goods. Therefore, she would "dwell with the English men, who loved her." She may have also told them about John Rolfe, for at this time, John wrote a letter to Governor Dale requesting permission to marry Pocahontas. She remained with the colonists, still a hostage.

John Rolfe, a religious man, had struggled against his attraction to the young Native American woman. Did God or the devil bring him "such diabolical assaults" that kept him awake at night wrestling his conscience, his love, his lust, "so daungerous an ulcer." How could he love Pocahontas, "whose education hath bin rude, her manners barbarous, her generation accursed"? How could he love someone so different in every way from himself?

John explained that Pocahontas shared his feelings. He wrote the governor of her "great apparance of love to me, her desire to be taught and instructed in the knowledge of God, her capablenesse of understanding, her aptnesse and willingnesse to receive anie good impression, and also the spirituall, besides her owne incitements stirring me up hereunto." So, for the glory of God, for the honor of Governor Dale, for "our Countreys good, the benefit of this Plantation, and for the converting of one unregenerate, to regeneration," John begged leave to wed the captive teenager.

John's conscience eased considerably with Pocahontas's baptism into the Christian faith. She was given the Biblical name Rebecca. How much she truly accepted Christianity is unknown. With Powhatan's consent, and in the presence of her uncle and other Powhatans, the couple wed in Jamestown's church on April 5, 1614. Native oral histories say Powhatan sent his daughter a necklace of pearls gathered from Chesapeake Bay oyster beds.

Did Pocahontas love John Rolfe? He claimed she did. She'd been a hostage for over a year; how much freedom she had to choose her husband is unknown. But she did publicly accept his faith, and she did marry the man. Sir Thomas Dale wrote, "She lives . . . lovingly with him." Like political marriages among royalty in Europe, the marriage of John Rolfe and Pocahontas led to a general peace between natives and colonists in Virginia.

Now known as Rebecca Rolfe, Pocahontas continued to learn English, and she ran her husband's household with the help of a few servants. They prospered, and John was named a secretary of the colony. Several native women probably lived with them, maybe even half sisters of Pocahontas. There must have been times when the customs and culture of the other spouse vexed both husband and wife. John wrote that the English and natives had been made by the same creator from the same mold. Other times he noted that Native Americans "doe runn headlong, yea with joy, into distruction." An exact date is not known, but sometime around 1615 the couple had a baby boy they named Thomas.

In April 1616, the little family sailed on Samuel Argall's ship for England with Sir Thomas Dale and at least six Powhatans. They'd been sent on a public relations and goodwill visit to encourage investment in the struggling colony. One of the Native Americans was Pocahontas's brother-in-law, a priest named Uttamatomakin who, like Pocahontas, would serve as Powhatan's eyes and ears in England. As Virginia's coast shrank against the horizon, the 100 people on board faced a cramped voyage filled with seasickness and poor food for seven long weeks before landing at Plymouth in England.

From Plymouth they traveled to London, a city of 200,000 inhabitants. Pocahontas must have felt overwhelmed by the masses, the buildings—hovels and shops and markets and great stone Gothic cathedrals—by the horses and roads and bridges, by the pollution and smells of garbage. It was like viewing the underside of an ant colony, not the few on top that the Virginia tribes knew about but the writhing masses beneath, the thousands of un-guessed-at people living across the sea. She must have known in her heart that with such sheer, aggressive numbers, with such technologies, with all this only a voyage away, the lives of her own people had changed forever.

John Smith claimed he wrote to the queen, telling of Pocahontas's many favors to the colony, how "she next under God, was still the instrument to preserve this Colonie from death, famine and utter confusion." The Lady Pocahontas, Smith wrote Her Majesty, was a rare woman, who at "last rejecting her barbarous condition, was maried to an *English* Gentleman, with whom at this present she is in *England*; the first Christian ever of that Nation, the first *Virginian* ever spake *English*, or had a childe in mariage by an *Englishman*, a matter surely, . . . worthy a Princes understanding." Smith begged Queen Anne to ignore Pocahontas's rough beginnings and the lowliness of Rolfe's estate and "doe her some honour more than she can imagine."

There is no evidence that King James I and Queen Anne received Pocahontas at their glittering court, but she did meet the king at a Twelfth Night masque in January 1617, a lavish entertainment of music, dance, and theatrical spectacle, where John Chamberlain wrote she was well placed in a good seat denoting her status. Chamberlain also gossiped about the couple and seemed put out by John Rolfe's rise above his station. "Here is . . . no fayre Lady," wrote Chamberlain of Pocahontas, "and yet with her tricking up and high stile and titles you might thincke her and her worshipfull husband to be somebody."

Samuel Purchas recorded that the bishop of London "entertained her with festival state and pomp beyond what I have seen in his greate hospitalitie afforded to other ladies." He also recalled the young woman's charm on Londoners at a succession of plays, balls, and public events, how she impressed people and "not only accustome her selfe to civilitie, but still carried her selfe as the Daughter of a King, and was accordingly respected." The Virginia Company arranged to pay Pocahontas four pounds per week for her upkeep and the fancy wardrobe necessary for society. At some point the couple moved from congested London to a country suburb.

Pocahontas reunited with John Smith while in England. He described a subdued greeting, not the joyous one he imagined, before Pocahontas turned away in silence, obscuring her face from view. "Not seeming well contented and in that humour," Smith, Rolfe, and others left her for two or three hours while she gathered her thoughts.

Smith recalled her words: "You did promise Powhatan what was yours should bee his, and he the like to you; you called him father being in his land a stranger, and by the same reason so must I doe you." For now she was a stranger in a strange land.

Smith interrupted, saying gallantly he mustn't let her call him father for she was a king's daughter.

Her face set sternly, Smith wrote, Pocahontas answered him: "You were . . . not afraid to come into my father's Countrie, and cause feare in him and all his people (but mee) and [yet] . . . feare you here I should call you father. I tell you then I will, and you shall call mee childe, and so I will bee for ever and ever your Countrieman." Couldn't he see she was English now, baptized, dressed in English clothes, living in an English house, married to an English man?

"They did tell us always you were dead," she said, "and I knew no other till I came to Plimoth." But Powhatan had asked Uttamatomakin to seek Smith out, "and know the truth, because your Countriemen will lie much," she told Smith.

A 1624 print, based on Van de Passe's 1617 portrait of Pocahontas.
Library of Congress LC-USZ62-8104

The Virginia Company commissioned the Dutch German engraver Simon Van de Passe to sketch a portrait of the young woman, making Pocahontas—a "civilized savage"—the poster girl for Jamestown and the company of investors. It is the only drawing known of Pocahontas done from life. Van de Passe made an engraving from his sketch, which could be printed and circulated.

Pocahontas is dressed as an English noblewoman, and perhaps mindful of the English perception of naked savages, she is weighed down by clothes that show no skin but her face. Van de Passe did not make her features more European, as later romanticized images would do, but showed her high cheekbones and her dark eyes and hair.

She told Van de Passe she was in her 21st year. Beneath the portrait in Latin, perhaps at Pocahontas's urging, it reads: "Matoaka als [also] Rebecka daughter to the mighty Prince Powhatan Emperour of Attanoughskomouch als Virginia converted and baptized in the Christian faith, and wife to the worthy Mr. Joh. Rolff."

After seven months in England, John Rolfe, Pocahontas, and baby Thomas prepared to sail for Virginia. But while the ship stopped at Gravesend, Pocahontas became ill, possibly from a sudden case of pneumonia or a worsening of something she already suffered from, like tuberculosis. It also may have been dysentery, known as the bloody flux—when Rolfe's ship returned to Jamestown it carried that disease with it.

Rolfe moved Pocahontas to an inn for her comfort, and there she died, perhaps only 21 years old. John buried his young wife on March 21, 1617, at St. George Church in Gravesend. When he sailed for Virginia, little Thomas, who'd also been ill, remained behind. John's brother would care for his nephew and see he received a proper English education. Father and son never saw one another again, though Thomas Rolfe one day returned to

Virginia. Powhatan mourned his daughter's death and longed to see her little son.

Pocahontas's story has been retold, revised, and reenvisioned over 400 years. She must have been bright, lively, curious, and brave, and deserving of her place as one of the most famous women of colonial America. In July 2006, in anticipation of the 400th anniversary of Jamestown's founding, a delegation of Virginia Native Americans visited England. At St. George Church in Gravesend they held a private ceremony for the tribal people, laden with emotion and tears. In the spot where Pocahontas's bones rest, they reclaimed this native daughter to her heritage.

Cecily Jordan Farrar
"Ancient Planter" of Virginia

THE SURVIVORS AT JAMESTOWN Fort had barely weathered the dark winter months of 1609–1610 known as the starving time. With each despairing week people watched their numbers dwindle until out of 500 colonists, an unimaginable 60 remained alive. In June 1610, they decided to abandon the colony and had already sailed up the James River when they met rescue ships carrying fresh colonists and supplies. The starved colonists, some of them unhappily, returned to Jamestown with the newcomers.

Then, in late August 1610, three more packed English vessels arrived in the Chesapeake. The ships, *Swan, Tryall,* and *Noah*, carried 250 passengers and a year's worth of provisions for Jamestown. On board one of the new ships—the *Swan*—waited a girl called Cecily, about 10 years old. The historical record remains silent on whether she sailed with parents or guardians. Even Cecily's last name is uncertain.

It must have been a shocking sight to enter the stockade, especially for a child. During those horrible months of famine, survivors had been too weak and ill to keep up the enclosed village. Much of the fort grounds had been used as a graveyard. How Cecily survived at Jamestown, who she lived with, or what she did, is unknown. Surely, at first, she faced the same dangers the colony had always struggled against: food rations, rough conditions, illness, humidity, heat, and continued skirmishes with the surrounding native tribes that often pinned the English behind the fort's log walls. Somehow Cecily survived. Perhaps in 1614 she even witnessed the marriage of Pocahontas and John Rolfe at the church centered in the stockade.

Once of age, and being a rare single female, Cecily would not have remained unwed. Sometime around 1616 when she was 16 or 17 she married a man named Bailey. Though scant, the historical record shows the couple had a daughter they named Temperance the following year.

It had been nine years since the first colonists established the fort at Jamestown. More people had arrived, and with larger numbers hungry for land, they'd established scattered farms along the James River and other rivers flowing to the Chesapeake. Cecily's young family joined the others creating little strongholds that encroached ever farther onto the lands of Virginia's native people. The marriage was short—Mr. Bailey died around 1619 when Temperance was three years old. He left Cecily a very young widow and bequeathed his 200 acres to the child.

A woman wasn't long without a husband in colonial America. Within a year Cecily married her neighbor, a longtime widower named Samuel Jordan, 25 years older than his new bride. They lived on a farm called Beggar's Bush, later known as Jordan's Journey. Cecily, Samuel, and Temperance, along with servants and probably a few others, lived within a fortified stockade, providing some safety from Native American attacks. About 10 houses, barns, and outbuildings hugged the stockade walls and crowded the enclosed space. In May 1621 Cecily and Samuel had a daughter, Mary. Both Cecily and Samuel were noted as "ancient planters" who had lived in the colony since the early days and were entitled to land. Samuel was granted 450 acres; Cecily, 100 acres.

Settlement farms like Jordan's Journey contributed to the mistrust, tension, and escalating anger among Virginia's tribal people. It's possible Samuel and Cecily were warned of the attacks planned for March 22, 1622, when allied forces of Virginia tribes struck the plantations up and down the James River. The Native American strategy was simple: a friendly approach followed by a sudden and overwhelming deadly ambush. Warriors killed anyone they could, dismembered victims, smashed, burned, and looted before vanishing back into the forests.

The Native Americans didn't risk their lives taking on strongholds where the colonists fought back, and perhaps this

A 1628 woodcut of the attack on March 22, 1622. Mathaeus Merian after Theodore de Bry. *Wikimedia Commons*

happened at Jordan's Journey, where Cecily and her family survived. About one-fourth of the colony's European population died that day, between 350 and 400 people. For Cecily, huddled with her young children at Jordan's Journey, it must have been a terrifying time. The next day a neighbor, William Farrar, fled to the Jordans. Eleven people at his farm had been killed, and he sought safety within Jordan's Journey's stockade. William remained at the Jordan plantation, and when Samuel Jordan died in March 1623, William stayed on and managed the plantation.

Samuel Jordan's body had barely touched the sod when the man who buried him, the Reverend Grivell Pooley, proposed to Cecily. Pregnant with her dead husband's child, and with two other small daughters to care for, Cecily agreed to wed the 46-year-old reverend a mere three or four days after her husband's death. But according to one story she set a condition: the contract must be kept secret until after she'd had the baby. Cecily gave birth to Samuel's daughter Margaret in 1623.

Meanwhile, Grivell did not abide by Cecily's wishes and bragged about snagging the lovely and vivacious Widow Jordan for his wife. Cecily turned around and accepted another proposal of marriage—from William Farrar. Whatever her reason for spurning the engagement to Grivell, Cecily found herself accused of breach of promise, the first breach of promise case to be heard in America.

In June 1623 Grivell pled his case before the governor and his council. Witnesses testified about the marriage contract between Grivell and Cecily. Captain Isack Maddeson swore that he'd been present when Grivell spoke words like a marriage ceremony to Cecily:

I Grivell Pooley take thee Sysley to my wedded wife, to have and to hold till death us depart and there to I plight thee my troth. Then (holding her by the hand) he spake these words I Sysley take thee Grivell to my wedded husband, to have and to hold till death us depart; but this examinant heard not her say any of those words, neither doth he remember that Mr. Pooley asked her whether she did consent to those words or that she did answer ant [any] things which he understood. then Mr. Pooley and she drank each to other and he kissed her and spake these words, I am thine and thou art mine till death us separate. Mrs. Jordan then desired that it might not be revealed that she did so soon bestow her love, after her husbands' death; whereupon Mr. Pooley promised before God that he would not reveal it, till she thought the time fitting.

The governor and council dithered and referred the case to the Virginia Company's council in London, which discussed the case at the end of April 1624. The London council could not decide what to do with the case either. The Virginia Assembly did, however, pass a law to protect the colony's bachelors, giving Cecily Jordan her footnote of fame in Virginia's legal history. No woman could promise herself to two men at the same time—this was against church law. All promises of marriage had to be reported to the council or the local church parish.

The fact that William Farrar remained in the Widow Jordan's household during the breach of promise suit added a delicious note of scandal that neighbors happily gossiped about. Living together out of wedlock was illegal, and authorities looked into the matter. Grivell Pooley appeared before the court and commented that the couple lived scandalously together. William frequented "her company alone without some body else to be in place according to the order of the court."

Nathaniel Causey, who lived at Jordan's Journey, testified he had never seen Mrs. Jordan and Mr. Farrar "indulge in unfitting or suspicious familiarities," but he had seen them kiss. Nathaniel also reported "a fearful thing fallen to Mrs. Jordan" that seemed to indicate a degree of guilt. Cecily had a vision. Two hands appeared—one clamped upon her head, the other on the head of her daughter while a voice repeated the word "Judgement . . . judgement . . ." Cecily declared "she was as broad awake as I am now," testified Causey.

In the end, with no decision from the council in Virginia or in London, Grivell gave up his claim on Cecily. He certainly did not have a claim on her affections.

> I Grevell Pooly preacher of the word do for myself freely acquit and discharge Mrs. Cycelie Jordan from all former contracts, promises and conditions made by her to me in a way of marriage and do bind myself in five hundred pounds never to have any claim right or title to her that way. In witness whereof I have hereunto set my hand and seal this third day of January 1624/25.

Finally, with the breach of promise suit and the scandal behind them, Cecily, age 25, wed William Farrar, age 42, on May 2, 1625. During the marriage Cecily gave birth to three more children, two sons and a daughter. After a few years, the couple moved to William's plantation on Farrar's Island.

William Farrar died in 1637. Cecily may have still been alive, but her name vanishes from the historical records after 1631. She'd been a founding woman at the first successful English colony in America, outlasting hardships, husbands, war, and the colonial courts. Her legend speaks of a flirtatious, vibrant, and well-liked young woman, but her real legacy is that she survived.

3

Goodwives to New England

> "A woman has been the breeder and nourisher of all these distempers."
>
> —John Winthrop, governor of Massachusetts Bay Colony, writing about Anne Hutchinson, 1644

FIVE HUNDRED MILES NORTH of Virginia, in December 1620, just over 100 passengers gathered on the *Mayflower*'s deck. They'd been at sea for three months, the ship crowded to near bursting, and now the 29 women and girls on board were as anxious as the men to glimpse their new home. Elizabeth Hopkins and Susannah White cradled infants in their arms, babies born during the voyage from England. The Massachusetts shoreline appeared a "hideous and desolate wilderness." What raced through their minds? Unlike the majority of women who traveled to Virginia—young and alone—the women of the *Mayflower* had dutifully followed husbands or fathers into the wilderness.

THE PILGRIMS OF PLYMOUTH

The *Mayflower* passengers established England's second colony, called Plymouth, in Massachusetts. About half of them were separatists. Once members of the Protestant Church of England, they believed that the church had slipped into corruption and failed to do away with the old Roman Catholic rituals. Separating themselves from the English church, many explored religious freedom in Holland for more than a decade before making the bold decision to come to America. Because of the dangerous voyage and uncertain future, some parents had left their small children behind with relatives in Europe. Many goodwives— the title of a married woman—on board the *Mayflower* must have felt anguish, not knowing whether they'd ever see their children again.

Those first weeks, most women and children remained on board the *Mayflower*, going ashore to wash clothes or gather for church services. The men prepared crude shelters and made first contact with the Wampanoag tribe. When the Englishmen stumbled across an empty native village while scouting the area, they were not above robbing the villager's homes. "Some of the best things we took away with us," recorded William Bradford, colony leader.

Like the Jamestown settlers, the Plymouth colonists faced a horrendous beginning. Tragedy struck early. Mary Allerton gave birth to a stillborn son. Dorothy Bradford fell overboard and drowned. Disease claimed the weak and sick as easy victims. William Bradford wrote:

> Being the depth of winter, and wanting houses and other comforts; being infected with the scurvie and other diseases, which this long vioage [voyage] . . . had brought upon them . . . that of 100 and odd people, scarce 50 remained. And of these in the time of most distres, ther was but 6 or 7 sound persons.

The Landing of the Pilgrims, December 22, 1620, Currier and Ives print, c. 1876. *Library of Congress, LC-USZ62-3461*

Four months later, in April 1621, Susannah White, Mary Brewster, Elizabeth Hopkins, and Eleanor Billington formed a tiny circle of the sole women survivors. Joined by a few teenage girls, among them Priscilla Mullins and Desire Minter, the handful of Plymouth females cooked, mended, and washed for all the colonists and cared for the children left motherless or orphaned. Like Jamestown, Plymouth clung to life with aid from Native Americans and the happy arrival of ships carrying new supplies and fresh colonists.

But the women resented this heavy burden of communal work. Before long, every family was granted its own parcel of land. This resulted in "very good success." Bradford observed:

> The women now went willingly into the field, and took their little ones with them to set corn; which before . . . to have compelled [forced] would have been thought great tyranny and oppression. . . . For men's wives to be commanded to do service for other men, as dressing

meat, washing their clothes, etc., they deemed it a kind of slavery, neither could many husbands well brook it.

THE PURITANS OF MASSACHUSETTS BAY

In March 1630, Margaret Winthrop bid farewell to her husband, John, as he prepared to leave England leading a wave of colonists bound for Massachusetts Bay. Margaret—whom John called "my sweet soule"—would not see her husband again for a year and a half. Husband and wife promised that on "mundayes [Monday] and frydayes [Friday] at 5: of the clocke at night, we shall meet in spirit till we meet in person."

The Winthrops were Puritans. Like the colonists at Plymouth, Puritans had also broken with the Church of England. They'd faced decades of threats and imprisonment for criticizing the English government and Anglican Church. In America, they hoped to create their own pure church, a new spiritual community based on the Bible's teachings. In his sermon, "A Model of Christian Charity," John Winthrop expressed hope that their "city on a hill" would shine as a beacon for others to follow.

After 78 days at sea, the great migration of 1,000 new settlers arrived in Massachusetts Bay. Although weak from scurvy and dysentery, they set to work immediately with Puritan gusto. Small towns rose in the wilderness, circling Boston Harbor. Settlers opened trade with Native Americans, doing brisk business for corn and fish. When the ship *Arabella* sailed for England to fetch emergency supplies, it carried 80 people who'd decided to abandon this harsh new life in Massachusetts.

For Puritans such as John Winthrop, however, the very founding of the Massachusetts Bay Colony honored God. Every hardship served as a welcome test from the Lord; the faithful embraced these tests and met them head-on. In November 1631 Margaret Winthrop and the couple's eight children finally joined John in Massachusetts.

During the 1630s and 1640s, thousands of Puritans fled England for Massachusetts Bay. The area—known as New England—expanded into a land of settled towns, small farms, and frontier outposts. Yet the process of uprooting, of leaving family and community in England, remained difficult.

WEETAMOO, A MOST HORRIBLE LAMENTATION

Many Puritans viewed their conflicts with Native Americans as another test of the Puritan experiment. They had little doubt they would prevail. From 1636 to 1637, the Puritans successfully waged an aggressive war on the Pequot tribe in Connecticut, killing hundreds of people and selling captives into slavery in the Caribbean West Indies. William Bradford described how the English set one Pequot village aflame:

> Those that scaped the fire were slaine with the sword; some hewed to peeces, others rune throw [run through] with their rapiers, so as they were quickly dispatchte, and very few escaped. It was conceived they thus destroyed about 400. at this time. It was a fearfull sight to see them thus frying in the fyer [fire], and the streams of blood quenching the same, and horrible was the stinck and sente [scent] ther of.

Bradford saw God's hand in this, for God had trapped the Pequot and "wrought so wonderfully for them [the Puritans] ... and give them so speedy a victory." The Puritans hailed their overwhelming victory as a triumph for God's chosen people.

In 1675 and 1676 Puritans and Native Americans again waged war, a bloody conflict that marked the last great effort by the native people of southern New England to drive the colonists out. The conflict spread across New England, the tribal people led by Metacom, a Wampanoag the English called King Philip.

Under his leadership the Wampanoag, Nipmuck, Pocumtuch, and a wary ally, the Narragansett, together destroyed 12 English frontier settlements.

Among those joining Metacom was a Native American woman named Weetamoo, meaning "sweet heart." Born around 1640 to the Pocasset people, a tribe of the Wampanoag, she led 300 warriors against the English.

Weetamoo had grown up in a household with only one sister. At her mother's side she learned the traditional skills native women needed to assure survival—cooking, preparing food for winter months, and tanning animal hides for clothing. But as the eldest child, she trained like a son to take her father's place as sachem, or chief. Like any native boy, she learned to hunt, swim, and fish. Weetamoo learned the diplomatic skills necessary for a leader. Around age 14 she experienced a vision quest, a ritual usually reserved for males, which sent her into the forest, fasting for days until her "child soul" had died and she emerged a new person.

Weetamoo's first husband, Wamsutta, was a son of the great Wampanoag sachem Massasoit and was Metacom's brother. In 1662 Wamsutta had gone to meet with the English about broken treaty promises when he fell ill and died. Weetamoo and Metacom believed the English had poisoned him.

Weetamoo married several more times, including a Narragansett sachem named Quinapin. During the war a captured Englishwoman named Mary Rowlandson lived in Weetamoo's household. Mary had no sense of Weetamoo's tragedies—the native woman lost a child during the war—and Mary dismissed Weetamoo as a "severe and proud Dame" who adorned herself with makeup and jewelry.

On August 6, 1676, the English ambushed Weetamoo's people. Her husband Quinapin, Metacom, Weetamoo's sister, and her nephew were all captured. Most of the warriors lay dead as Weetamoo tried to escape. She drowned trying to cross the

Taunton River. When the English retrieved her body, they cut off her head and displayed it on a pike. "The Indians who were prisoners there, knew it presently [immediately]," wrote Increase Mather, a minister, "and made a most horrible and diabolical Lamentation, crying out that it was their Queens head." The English sold Weetamoo's sister and her son into slavery in the West Indies. Metacom, who escaped, was later recaptured and killed. The English killed Quinapin on August 25.

IN GOD'S GRACE

Politics and social life blended with religion in Massachusetts Bay Colony. Political power rested with those men who owned property and were elected as full members into the Puritan church. When Puritans gathered for worship, the congregation sat according to wealth, sex, and even age.

Puritans believed women, like men, could receive God's grace and attain membership in the church, but equality ended there. During daylong services, women crammed onto church benches with their children wedged beside them and babies sitting on their laps, separated from male worshippers. No women were ministers, no women held church office, no women signed church covenants. Women had no voice in the selection of new ministers.

Although officially powerless, New England women wielded some influence behind the scenes. A few well-placed words from female parishoners could ruin a minister's reputation. When Jeremiah Shepard lost his position, he blamed Goodwife Elithorp, claiming she hated him. "If she had an opportunity he doubted not but she would cut his throat," recorded retired minister Samuel Phillips. Shepard also faced opposition from Phillips's wife. The steely matron quietly spread the word that young Jeremiah seriously neglected his studies.

Women's voices were often heard through their husbands, who pushed church elders to set up new churches in outlying areas. Women nursing babies and raising a house full of young ones had a hard time walking miles into town to attend church. In winter, many women could not attend church at all. John Winthrop described the ordeal of Mrs. Dalkin, who nearly drowned crossing a swollen river on her way to church. Her husband, who could not swim, helplessly watched his wife flail in the water. Fortunately, the family dog was made of sterner stuff—the animal plunged into the water, where "She caught hold on the dog's tail, so he drew her to shore and saved her life," Winthrop noted in his journal.

One outlying parish wrangled with the town of Ipswich over a new church and minister. A local church history related the event:

> While we were in this great conflict . . . som women without the knowledge of theire husbands, and with the advice of some few men went to other towns and got help and raised the house that we intended for a meeting house [church] if we could git liberty.

For their part in establishing this new church, three wives were charged with contempt of authority.

DISSENTERS

No woman in the Puritan world would dare preach, but then along came Anne Hutchinson. When she preached to gatherings of men and women in her home, the punishment fell swift and sure—in 1638 leaders excommunicated and banished Anne from the colony.

After the Hutchinson case, Puritan authorities cracked down even harder on religious dissenters. When they punished Sarah Keayne for preaching in "mixed assembly" of men and women, her husband claimed she had "unwifed herself."

Anne Hutchinson preaching to men and women in her home, 1637.
Painted by Howard Pyle, circa 1901.
Library of Congress, LC-USZ62-53343

The Quakers, another religious group, disregarded the need
for ministers altogether. They believed each person possessed
an "inner light" that communicated directly with God. In 1658,
Mary Dyer, a follower of Anne Hutchinson, returned to Boston as a Quaker. Puritan authorities quickly suppressed this
heretical threat and hanged Mary on Boston Common in 1660.
In another part of Massachusetts, officials tied three Quaker
women to the back of a cart and whipped them as they stag-
gered in a procession winding from town to town.

"A VIRTUOUS WOMAN"

"Families . . . are the first foundation of Humane Societies," wrote Samuel Willard in *A Compleat Body of Divinity*, "and do . . . require there be Order in them, without which Mankind would fall." Within all colonial families, order meant the husband ruled over all as the master. His wife's place remained fastened on a lower rung, yet above her children and servants.

The title "notable housewife" rang as a sterling compliment for a colonial woman. A wife might temporarily transform into a "deputy husband" if her mate fell ill or left home on business and men's work needed doing. But she served first as a housewife who "worketh willingly with her hands" and "eateth not the bread of idelness."

Ministers looked no further than their heavy leather-bound Bibles for inspiration regarding the perfect woman. The model appeared in Proverbs 31. "Who can find a virtuous woman?" the proverb posed, "For her price is far above rubies." A virtuous woman proved a good neighbor and "stretcheth out her hand to the poor." She ruled as a good mistress, stern but kind, to her servants. She dressed with modesty, for "strength and honour are her clothing." And at heaven's gate, ended the proverb, "let her own works praise her."

Anne Hutchinson

"A Woman Unfit for Our Society"

"MISTRESS HUTCHINSON, YOU ARE called here as one of those that have troubled the peace of the commonwealth and the churches here."

John Winthrop's voice carried on the icy November air, permeating every corner of the meetinghouse in Cambridge, Massachusetts. Anne Marbury Hutchinson, age 46 and suffering through a difficult 16th pregnancy, stood in the center of the room. Crammed onto benches around the meetinghouse sat nearly 40 magistrates and ministers who would question, testify against, and judge her.

Anne's journey to this day—November 7, 1637—began several years before. Alongside her merchant husband, Will, and eleven of their children, she'd sailed from England to Massachusetts in 1634. They came as part of a great tide of Puritans first led to the New World by John Winthrop in 1630. Her old minister, teacher, and friend John Cotton had urged the Hutchinsons to join the Puritan migration.

The Massachusetts church had accepted Anne and Will into membership after reviewing evidence of their good behavior and hearing their public testimony of faith and conversion.

Anne Hutchinson faces the magistrates at her trial.
US History Images

Anne joined some of the women's prayer meetings in Boston. In her role as a midwife she often discussed the Bible with patients, offering wisdom and comfort to women fearing death in child-birth. In 1635 Anne began hosting a weekly women's meeting in her home to talk about scripture, theology, and salvation.

But by 1636 Anne's meetings transformed into something Puritan authorities viewed as potent and explosive. The gatherings swelled to include men. Anne commented, interpreted, and preached on church doctrine. She answered questions about scripture. She encouraged her followers to evaluate and question their ministers. She supported her brother-in-law, Reverend John Wheelwright, a man already censured by the court for his radical beliefs. The men confronting Anne in the Cambridge meetinghouse that day saw a dangerous threat to authority, a woman who dabbled in matters not befitting a female. There was something dark, they thought, something of the devil, in a woman so bold and sharp-tongued as Mistress Hutchinson.

John Winthrop demanded by what authority Anne set herself up to teach. "What hurt comes of this," he warned, "you will be guilty of."

Anne stood her ground: "Sir, I do not believe that to be so."

"Well, we see how it is," he replied. "We must therefore put it away from you or restrain you from maintaining this course. We are your judges, and not you ours."

"If you have a rule for it from God's own word you may," answered Anne. "If it please you by authority to put [my teaching] down, I will freely let you, for I am subject to your authority. I desire that you would then set me down a rule by which I may put them away [her followers] that come unto me and so have peace in doing so."

"Yes you are the woman of most note, and of best abilities," said Winthrop. He demanded once more by what authority "you take upon you to be such a public instructor."

At this point, Anne fainted. Her husband and a few supporters rushed to her side. The court offered her a bench and the
questions continued. Both Anne and her accusers knew the
Bible by heart and could quote scripture to support their cases.

Anne claimed a clear rule appeared in Titus that the elder
women should instruct the younger. She must have a time and
a place to do that. Winthrop turned the point around. Titus
held older women "may instruct the young women to be sober
minded, that they love their husbands, that they love their children. That they be temperate, chaste, keeping at home, good
and subject unto their husbands, that the word of God be not
evil spoken of." That was a far different thing than what Anne
taught.

Anne countered, "If any come to my house to be instructed
in the ways of God what rule have I to put them away? . . . Do
you think it not lawful for me to teach women and why do you
call me to teach the court?"

Winthrop snapped, "We do not call you to teach the court
but to lay open yourself." The bottom line, said Winthrop, was
that Anne's course proved dangerous to the state. She seduced
"honest persons that are called to those meetings and your
opinions, being known to be different from the word of God."

"Sir, I do not believe that to be so," said Anne.

Anne's meetings, charged Winthrop, encouraged trouble
when she questioned and faulted the town's ministers. Had
she not criticized many of them for teaching a covenant of
works, rather than a covenant of grace? Had she not claimed
the ministers were not able teachers of the New Testament?
Didn't Anne claim that only her friend Mr. Cotton proved a
true teacher?

Questions about the covenant of works and the covenant
of grace delved into the very heart of salvation for the Puritans. John Winthrop and the orthodox ministers believed God
selected a person's soul before birth for salvation. A person

granted this gift demonstrated their selection through faith and performing good works, by constant striving to cleanse the soul and lead a devout life. If a person followed the laws of church and state, he or she had some assurance of being one of the elect and saved.

Anne rejected this view of salvation, calling it a covenant of works. She held that only God's grace brought salvation— a covenant of grace. External works were not necessary, could even be deceptive. Anyone could go through the motions of good works while lacking true grace, which she believed God granted freely without human effort or intervention.

While many Puritans anguished over their fate—wondering if God had saved them or cast them into the pits of hell—Anne Hutchinson felt confident she had received the Holy Spirit. She communed with God herself, without the aid of the ministers. Winthrop reported her saying: "Here is a great stir about graces and looking to hearts, but give me Christ. I seek not for graces, but for Christ."

The ministers saw this as encouragement for people to do nothing and still expect salvation. If Anne were right, there would be no need to read the Bible, attend church, or follow rules. Such thinking appealed to those labeled "profane persons" looking for an easy route to heaven, "to see nothing, to have nothing, but wait for Christ to do all."

Deputy Governor Thomas Dudley noted that all was peaceful in the colony until Mrs. Hutchinson arrived. She had spread her "strange opinions" and given rise to factions. And, "if she in particular hath disparaged all our ministers in the land that they have preached a covenant of works, and only Mr. Cotton a covenant of grace, why this is not to be suffered." They must "take away the foundation" of Anne's ideas so that "the building will fall."

"I pray, Sir," said Anne, "prove it that I said they preached nothing but a covenant of works."

Winthrop asked the ministers who had visited Anne and questioned her to testify. Many spoke reluctantly and only on the court's order. They reported Anne had indeed said they preached a covenant of works and only John Cotton preached a covenant of grace. Anne said they were not good teachers of the New Testament.

Anne denied this. "Prove that I said so," she responded. She only claimed to have discussed such things in private conversations with the ministers, and only public acts mattered in court.

Dudley, clearly frustrated, told her: "What do I do charging of you if you deny what is so fully proved?"

Winthrop summarized the six ministers' testimony and finished, "It appears plainly that you have spoken it, and whereas you say that it was drawn from you in a way of friendship, you did profess then that is was out of conscience that you spoke."

By now dusky shadows filled the meetinghouse. Winthrop adjourned court until the next morning, granting Anne more time to consider and acknowledge her errors so that she "might be reduced [corrected]."

The next day Anne asked that the ministers testify under oath, which caused great wrangling, as the ministers opposed the idea. Winthrop noted that Anne's derogatory statements about the ministers weakened "the hands and hearts of the people towards them. . . . And this was spoken not, as was pretended, out of private conference but out of conscience."

The court called Anne's teacher, the Reverend John Cotton, to testify. He had encouraged many of Anne's beliefs. A popular preacher, he avoided conflict and now walked a fine line as he tried to support Anne without hurting himself.

On Anne's statements that the other ministers "did not hold forth a covenant of grace as I did," Cotton recalled, "I told her I was very sorry that she put comparisons between my ministry and theirs, . . . and I had rather that she had put us in fellowship with them and not have made that discrepancy." Nor did the ministers, at the time they questioned her, seem very bothered, not like they claimed to be now. Indeed, they had told Anne they wouldn't "so easily believe reports as they had done" and "would speak no more of it."

At this point, there was little Winthrop and Dudley could do with Anne. She had deflected their questions, denied the charges, refused to answer. What things she had said, she claimed were spoken in private conversations and not in public.

But then, at her moment of victory, Anne started talking, a rush of words as she stood before the magistrates. Perhaps she knew this was her one chance to have her views recorded. As a woman she had no public role, no voice, no vote, no say in any matter. So Anne did what she should not have done—she lectured the judges on her spiritual journey. Her words, scribbled down in the meetinghouse, gave her a voice no other woman in 17th-century America possessed.

Anne began back in England where, troubled at the "falseness of the . . . Church there . . . I set apart a day of solemn humiliation and pondering of the thing by myself, to seek direction from God." This perked her judges' ears, who believed most women lacked the brainpower to resolve such weighty matters. Then Anne divulged that God revealed passages of scripture to her. "He had led me see which was the clear ministry and which was the wrong. Since that time [in England], I confess, I have been more . . . careful whom I heard [preach]." This was one of the reasons the Hutchinsons came to America—to follow John Cotton and John Wheelwright.

Winthrop held his tongue. Every word from Anne's lips proved her threat to the state. He later wrote that Anne talked of "God's dealing with her, and how He revealed himself to her, and made her know what she had to do."

Perhaps realizing she'd said too much, Anne finished: "Now, if you do condemn me for speaking what in my conscience I know to be truth, I must commit myself unto the Lord."

Questions filled the meetinghouse. How did she know God's spirit talked to her? asked Increase Nowell, a court assistant.

"How did Abraham know that it was God that bid him offer his son?" replied Anne.

"By an immediate voice?" asked Dudley, meaning the direct voice of God.

"So to me, by an immediate revelation," Anne agreed.

"How an immediate revelation?" Dudley asked.

"By the voice of his own spirit to my soul," said Anne.

Ah, here was something the court could hang upon the elusive Mistress Hutchinson. Most Puritans believed revelation came through scripture interpreted by a minister. Anne claimed God had revealed himself directly to her, a claim considered a vain and arrogant boast for a woman—she placed herself on an equal plane with her betters, the ministers.

"Then the Lord did reveal himself to me, sitting upon a throne of justice," said Anne, and he told her she "must come to New England, yet I must not fear nor be dismayed."

"I will give you one place more which the Lord brought to me by immediate revelations," continued Anne, "and that doth concern you all. It is in Daniel 6 when the president [king] could find nothing against Daniel, because he was faithful, they fought against him concerning the law of his God, to cast him into the lion's den. So it was revealed to me that they should plot against me. But the Lord bid me not to fear, for he that delivered Daniel . . . his hand was not shortened. And see! This scripture fulfilled this day in mine eyes!"

Later, the Reverend Thomas Weld wrote that he found Anne "so fierce" she was more like "the lions after they were let loose," than Daniel.

"Therefore," warned Anne, "take heed how you proceed against me. For you have no power over my body. Neither can you do me any harm, for I am in the hands of the eternal Jehovah my Saviour . . . and I do verily believe that he will deliver me out of your hands." She knew what they planned to do with her and promised, "God will ruin you and your posterity, and this whole state."

Anne also claimed a gift of prophecy—the power to know the future based on her study of scripture. People believed prophecy, astrology, portents, and signs worked in their world. But Anne's claim made her "raised up of God" and brought followers to her doorstep. Only ministers, only men, had this gift.

Winthrop now spoke, brushing aside Anne's revelations as "delusion."

"The ground work of her revelations is the immediate revelation of the spirit and not by the ministry of the words," he said. By this means she had "very much abused the country." Dudley then linked Anne's revelations to the religious extremism that had swept Germany with violence. "Whether the Devil may inspire the same in their hearts here I know not," said Dudley, "for I am fully persuaded that Mistress Hutchinson is deluded by the Devil."

The court conferred before the governor pronounced Anne's fate. "Mistress Hutchinson, the sentence of the court you hear is that you are banished from our jurisdiction as being a woman unfit for our society, and are to be imprisoned till the court shall send you away."

"I desire to know wherefore I am banished?" said Anne.

"Say no more," Winthrop told her. "The court knows wherefore and is satisfied."

That long, cold winter Anne lived under house arrest at the home of Joseph Weld, brother of the Reverend Thomas Weld. Anne's youngest children were too little to brave the freezing two-mile walk to visit. She spent her days studying scripture, her pregnancy growing heavier. Ministers filled the Weld house; they came to question Anne and write down the "errors, taken from her own mouth."

In the meantime, the government acted against many of Anne's supporters—mostly merchants and businessmen, throwing them in jail, stripping away their right to vote, and levying heavy fines against them. In reaction to this antinomian crisis (a label Winthrop gave it, meaning against or opposed to law) colony leaders established a college to train orthodox ministers and protect against further threats. John Harvard provided most of the funds needed for the new college that bore his name.

On Thursday, March 15, Anne entered her church in Boston. Again she faced a room of men prepared to judge her. Her family had until the end of March to leave the colony for Rhode Island, established in 1636 by Roger Williams after his banishment from Massachusetts. Will Hutchinson had already gone ahead to prepare a new home. But before Anne's banishment, the church demanded she deny her heresies or face excommunication.

The church court read the list of more than 30 errors compiled against Anne. Were these opinions held by Sister Hutchinson or not, asked the court.

"If this be error," said Anne, "then it is mine and I ought to lay it down. If it be truth, it is not mine but Christ Jesus', and then I am not to lay it down." She complained that church elders had visited her in private and asked these questions, swearing they had not come to "entrap nor ensnare me." Yet, now her words were "stated publicly in the church." Anne claimed she only questioned these things but "did not hold diverse of these things I am accused of."

Anne quoted scripture, trying to define her beliefs on the soul and salvation, life after death, and God's meanings. Testimony dragged on for hours. She made some concessions to her judges and other times fought their pressure to change her views.

Anne's opinions, claimed John Davenport, shook the very foundation of the Puritan faith, while the Reverend John Eliot feared for her soul. Surely, her inquisitors believed, Anne was not guided by God but by her own pride. "She is of a most dangerous spirit," warned Thomas Shepard, "and likely with her fluent tongue and forwardness in expression to seduce and draw away many—especially simple women of her own sex." Those few who rose and defended Anne, including her son Edward and son-in-law Thomas Savage, were warned they too would be found out by God.

Hardest for Anne, her old minister and teacher John Cotton warned her female followers they did not receive the truth from Anne, "For, you see, she is but a woman," he said. Cotton had quietly distanced himself from Anne. Before the church, he warned her to consider, "how the dishonor you have brought unto God by these unsound tenets of yours is far greater than all the honor you have brought to Him. And the evil of your opinions doth outweigh all the good of your doings." Anne must "consider how many poor souls you have misled." She'd done "the uttermost to raze the very foundation of religion to the ground, and to destroy our faith."

The final dagger was his sly slander that "and though I have not heard—neither do I think—you have been unfaithful to your husband in his marriage covenant, yet that will follow upon it. . . . And so more dangerous evils and filthy uncleanness and other sins will follow than you do now imagine or conceive."

The next day, under Cotton's guidance, Anne confessed many of her errors or answered, "I never held any such thing." She spoke phrases of contrition: "I do acknowledge I was deeply deceived; the opinion was very dangerous. . . . I acknowledge my mistake." She apologized for slighting the ministers.

But Anne Hutchinson might have saved her breath. Her judges declared she was not truly sorry and penitent. The pileup began. Reverend Hugh Peter warned Anne, "You have stepped out of your place. You have rather been a husband than a wife; and a preacher than a hearer; and a magistrate than a subject . . . you have not been humbled for this."

"I look at her as a dangerous instrument of the Devil," said another, "raised up by Satan amongst us to raise up divisions and contentions. . . . And the misgovernment of this woman's tongue hath been a great cause of this disorder, which hath been to set up herself and to draw disciples after her. . . . Therefore, we should sin against God if we should not put away from us so evil a woman, guilty of such foul evils."

Reverend Wilson delivered Anne's punishment. "In the name of our Lord Jesus Christ and in the name of the church, I do not only pronounce you worthy to be cast out, but I do cast you out. And in the name of Christ, I do deliver you up to Satan, that you may learn no more to blaspheme, to seduce, and to lie."

Anne stood up. "The Lord judges not as man judges," she told the filled church. "Better to be cast out of the church than to deny Christ." She strode from the church, hand in hand with her friend and supporter Mary Dyer.

On April 1, 1638, as cold weather still gripped New England, Anne, eight of her children, and a number of her supporters, both men and women, began the six-day walk to the new settlement of Portsmouth, Rhode Island. Twenty-four-year-old Edward Hutchinson helped his pregnant mother and his siblings—the youngest, Zuriel, was only two—on the difficult journey.

The families settled at Portsmouth, establishing houses, farms, and communal grazing lands around Great Cove. In June, about six weeks early, Anne began labor. She delivered not a baby but a mass of undeveloped tissue that appeared like bunches of slimy grapes. Known today as a hydatidiform mole, this rare condition occurs when a fertilized egg develops as an abnormal cluster of cells instead of a normal embryo.

When news of Anne's tragedy reached Massachusetts, Winthrop rejoiced, "See how the wisdom of God fitted this judgment to her sin every way, for look—as she had vented misshapen opinions, so she must bring forth deformed monsters."

To Winthrop, Anne's delivery confirmed her link with the devil and her punishment as a heretic.

Winthrop kept his ears open for news of Anne and refused to let her settle in peace. In February 1640 he sent three ministers to pressure her to recant her views. When they arrived on Anne's doorstep she cried, "From the Church of Boston? I know no such church, neither will I own it. You may call it the 'Whore and Strumpet of Boston,' but no church of Christ." After that reception, the ministers sought Will's help to soften his wife. But he cut them off. "I am more nearly tied to my wife than to the church," he told them. "I do think her to be a dear saint and servant of God."

When her beloved husband died at age 55, Anne retreated from society. Once more ministers from Boston descended upon her, and once more she refused to recant. They warned Anne that Massachusetts might soon take over Rhode Island. Boldly, Anne decided to move yet again, this time leaving New England behind for a new home in the Dutch colony of New Amsterdam. In the summer of 1642, at age 51, she moved her family to a meadow beside Pelham Bay.

Anne had never feared the Native Americans living among and around the white settlers. Back in Boston she'd earned scorn from colony leaders for opposing their war against the Pequot. In the fall of 1643 Anne ignored warnings to flee her farm during tribal raids. On a warm fall day a war party of Siwanoy warriors fell upon Anne's homestead. Anne and six of her children were killed, scalped, and burned inside the farmhouse.

Back in Boston, church and colony leaders heralded Anne's death as another sign of God's retribution. Thomas Weld spoke for many: God picked "out this woeful woman" and "freed us from this great and sore affliction."

At a time when women proved their worth through a life of meek subservience, bright, literate, and bold Anne Hutchinson championed freedom of conscience, the rights of individuals to their beliefs, and the right to question authority. Like many 17th-century women, Anne did her duty, married, bore children, and ran her household. But she also went toe to toe with the leaders of early Massachusetts and paid dearly for her outspokenness.

Anne Dudley Bradstreet
Puritan Poet

WHAT ANNE BRADSTREET accomplished with her poetry was so rare for a woman in the 1600s that when her brother-in-law John Woodbridge published her writings in England as *The Tenth Muse* in 1650, he added an explanatory introduction. Woodbridge feared readers' "unbelief," their questioning "whether it be a woman's work, and ask, is it possible?" He assured people the poems had been written by a woman and praised Anne's feminine virtues, "her pious conversation, her courteous disposition, her exact diligence in her place."

He also included an apology to Anne. "I fear the displeasure of no person in the publishing of these Poems but the Authors, without whose knowledge, and contrary to her expectation, I have presumed to bring to the publick view what she resolved should never in such a manner see the Sun." Woodbridge acknowledged that by publishing Anne's work, he'd denied her the chance to polish her poems with her "owne sweet hand." Indeed, Anne had intended her poems only for family and friends. She'd dedicated several to her father. One poem even ended with an apology for her verse. Following "The Foure Seasons of the Yeare," she wrote:

> *My Subjects bare, my Brains are bad,*
> *Or better Lines you should have had; . . . .*
> *The last, though bad, I could not mend,*
> *Accept therefore of what is penn'd,*
> *And all the faults which you shall spy,*
> *Shall at your feet for pardon cry.*
>   *Your dutifull Daughter, A. B.*

The Tenth Muse is an epic work running several hundred pages. The collection includes "The Prologue" and five quaternions, poems with a single theme divided into four parts. "The Foure Elements" depicts a struggle between fire, air, earth and water, "Which was the strongest, noblest, the best, / Who the most good could shew, & who most rage / For to declare themselves they all ingage." In "Of the Foure humours in Mans constitution" Anne explores the role of choler (yellow bile), blood, phlegm, and melancholy (black bile), the four bodily fluids medicine had focused on since ancient Greece. In another, "The Foure Ages of Man" she begins "Loe now! Four other acts upon the stage, / Childhood, and Youth, the Manly and Old-age."

Anne introduces spring, "With smiling Sun-shine face, and garments green, / She gently thus began, like some fair Queen," in the quaternion "The four Seasons of the Yeare." In a mammoth work called "The Foure Monarchies" Anne traces the history of ancient Assyria, Persia, Greece, and Rome. But after 3,500 lines of iambic pentameter, Anne struggled to finish the last section. Most of Rome's story remains untold and ends in another apology from the author.

The Tenth Muse speaks to the excellent education Anne received. Within the poems she displays an understanding and knowledge of history, politics, Renaissance art, theology and the

Bible, medicine, classic literature of Greece and Rome, mythol-
ogy, astronomy, and astrology. As a group, Puritans believed
in education, and books played an important part in a Puritan
household. Yet even her education and the acceptance of her
writings within her own family did not mean the rest of the
world would accept Anne's work. In "The Prologue" she wrote:

> I am obnoxious to each carping tongue,
> Who says, my hand a needle better fits,
> A Poet's Pen, all scorne, I should thus wrong;
> For such despite they cast on Female wits:
> If what I doe prove well, it won't advance,
> They'l say its stolne, or else, it was by chance.

In the 1600s such an outpouring of literature usually flowed
from educated men sponsored by aristocratic patrons. Instead
this collection of formal poems spilled from the pen of a talented woman, a mother of eight children with a household to
manage in the frontier wilderness of New England.

What little is known of Anne's life is gleaned mostly from a
few pages she left for her children. She was born in 1612 or early
1613 in Northamptonshire, England. Her father, Thomas Dudley, managed the estates of the Earl of Lincoln, and the family
prospered. Anne suffered from a series of illnesses in childhood
and remained in poor health throughout her life. From her sick-
bed Anne wrestled with religious doubts and questioned God's
path for her, finally accepting and renewing her faith. Anne cir-
cled through this pattern many times in her life. Around age
14 or 15, "I found my heart more carnall," she wrote, "& sitting
loose from God, vanity & ye follyes of Youth take hold of me."

In 1621 Thomas Dudley hired Simon Bradstreet as an assistant, and though the parties separated a few years later, Simon
kept in touch with the Dudleys. Anne had turned 16 when God
"smott me" with smallpox. "I besought the Lord, & confessed

my pride and vanity." Her health restored, she wed Simon Bradstreet in 1628. Thomas Dudley may have arranged his daughter's marriage, but it turned out to be a love match.

In 1630 Simon and Anne sailed with her family on the *Arabella* to the fledgling Puritan settlement in Massachusetts. Anne
found "a new World and new manners at wch my heart rose."
The family faced shortages and illness that tested everyone's
resolve and, as usual during times of sickness and trouble, Anne
believed God sent trials to "hu[m]ble and try me & doe me
Good." At last she felt "convinced it was ye way of God, I submitted to it & joined to ye chh.[church], at Boston."

For more than four years Anne failed to conceive a child,
marking her as a failure to her contemporaries. "It pleased God
to keep me a long time without a child," she wrote, "wch was
a great grief to me, and cost me many prayers and tears." In
1632 she gave birth to her first child, Samuel, followed by seven
others: Dorothy, Sarah, Simon Jr., Dudley, Hannah, Mercy, and
John.

Over the years Anne and Simon moved to Newtown (Cambridge), then to Ipswich, Massachusetts, where Anne wrote most
of the poetry in *The Tenth Muse*, and finally settled in Andover.
The Dudleys and Bradstreets rose in the Puritan world. Both
Thomas Dudley and Simon Bradstreet served as governors of
Massachusetts, and Simon served as the colony's representative
in England. Anne wrote the poems for the *The Tenth Muse* starting in 1638 and through the 1640s.

Unlike the formal poems of *The Tenth Muse*, Anne's writings after 1650 often recounted events in her life, her religious
struggles, and her love of her family, husband, and children.
These were not published until after Anne's death. Illness and
lameness often kept Anne bedridden for months at a time. After
one bout of sickness, she wrote on August 28, 1656, "After much
weaknes & sicknes when my spirits were worn out, and many
times my faith weak likewise, the Lord was pleased to uphold

my drooping heart, and to manifest his love to me, and this is that wch stayes my soul."

Anne wanted her children to understand her religious journey. She freely confessed her own struggles before finding peace in both God and nature. "Many times hath Satan troubled me concerning ye verity [truth] of ye Scriptures," she wrote, and many times she wondered "whether there was a God, I never saw any miracles to confirm me, and those wch I read of how did [I] Know but they were feigned. That there is a God my Reason would soon tell me by the wondrous works that I see, the vast frame of ye Heaven + ye Earth, the order of all things night and day, Summer & Winter, Spring and Autumne, the dayly providing for this great household upon ye Earth, ye preserving + directing of All to its proper End."

Anne wrote *Meditations Divine and morall*, a rare manuscript surviving from 1664, dedicated to her son Simon Bradstreet, which contained 77 verses of her advice and observations. Number 4 reminded that "A ship that beares much saile & little or no ballast, is easily over set, and that man whose head hath great abilities and his heart little or no grace is in danger of foundering." Number 6 extols, "The finest bread hath the least bran the purest hon[e]y the least wax and the sincerest Christian the least self love."

Anne's love poems to her husband—"who is my chiefest comforter on Earth"—leave a vivid record of a marriage based on love, passion, and friendship. When Simon traveled to England on business, Anne compared herself to the winter earth, her husband the sun, as she hungers for his warm return. "I like the earth this season, mourn in black, / My Sun is gone so far in's Zodiack, / Whom whilst I joy'd, not storms, nor frosts I felt, / His warmth such frigid colds did cause to melt. / My chilled limbs now nummed lye forlorn; / Return, return sweet *Sol* from *Capricorn*." In another poem, one of her most famous, "To my Dear and loving Husband," Anne wrote:

A treasure of American literature, *Meditations Divine and morall*, in Anne Bradstreet's own hand.

If ever two were one, then surely we.
If ever man were lov'd by wife, then thee;
If ever wife was happy in a man,
Compare with me ye women if you can.
I prize thy love more than whole Mines of gold,
Or all the riches that the East doth hold.
My love is such that Rivers cannot quench.

Anne wrote poems marking the departure of loved ones overseas and celebrating their return. She wrote eulogies for both her parents. Too often she wrote poems in memory of her little grandchildren:

> *In memory of my dear grand-child Elizabeth*
> *Bradstreet, who deceased August, 1665*
> *being a year and half old:*

> *"Farewel dear babe, my hearts too much content,*
> *Farewel sweet babe, the pleasure of mine eye,*
> *Farewel fair flower that for a space was lent,*
> *Then ta'en away unto Eternity."*

On July 10, 1666, the Bradstreet home burned to the ground, awakening her "wth thundering nois / And piteous shrieks of dreadful voice." In a poem Anne recorded all she'd lost:

> *My pleasant things in ashes lye*
> *And them behold no more shall I.*
> *Under thy roof no guest shall sitt,*
> *Nor at they Table eat a bitt.*
> *No pleasant tale shall 'ere be told*
> *Nor things recounted done of old.*

Anne then chides herself, asking: "And did thy wealth on earth abide?" No, she thinks, "My hope, and Treasure lyes Above."

After years of declining health, Anne Bradstreet, the first female poet published in either England or America, died in Andover on September 16, 1672, a "weary pilgrim" ready to sleep. Talented, bright, and beloved, she wrote of her own ending:

> Oh how I long to be at rest,
> And soare on high among the blest.
> This body shall in silence sleep,
> Mine eyes no more shall ever weep.

The Captivity of
Mary Rowlandson

On the morning of February 10, 1676, Mary Rowlandson's husband, Joseph, a Puritan minister, was in Boston, desperately seeking military protection for their isolated frontier settlement of Lancaster, Massachusetts. About 50 families lived in Lancaster, and in times of danger they gathered in five or six garrison houses for protection. Fear had spread in the past months as raiding bands of Wampanoags, Narragansetts, Pocumtuchs, and Nipmucks, in a final stand to stop the surge of colonists onto native lands, had unleashed a brutal campaign that left scores of New England towns in flames. Wampanoag chief Metacom—called King Philip by the English—led the Native Americans. Frontier families like the Rowlandsons faced the brunt of the tribes' fury.

Not long after sunrise, Mary heard the thunder of gunshots. Massive plumes of black smoke marked her neighbors' burning homes. Before long warriors surrounded the Rowlandson homestead, hiding in the hills, sheltering behind trees and stones, shooting from inside the Rowlandsons' own barn. Bullets struck the house like a rain of hail.

When the warriors set fire to the house, using the Rowland-sons' store of flax and hemp as fuel, Mary and her family faced an agonizing decision. "Some in our house were fighting for their lives," she recorded, "others wallowing in their blood, the house on fire over our heads, and the bloody heathen ready to knock us on the head, if we stirred out." Mothers screamed, children cried. The fire roared, bullets rattled, "and the Indians gaping before us with their guns, spears, and hatchets to devour us."

As they tried to escape, Mary's brother-in-law and one of her sisters fell dead. Bullets broke the leg of her nephew. Warriors swooped in and finished the boy with their hatchets. A bullet pierced Mary's side, and another struck her daughter, Sarah, held in Mary's arms. Of the 37 people at the Rowlandson farm, 12 lay dead. The warriors took the others captive, including Mary, nearly 40 years old, her daughters Sarah and Mary, aged 6 and 10, and her 14-year-old son, Joseph, marching the prisoners west and north into the wilderness. Mary, who had often said she would rather die than be taken captive, marveled that in her moment of trial, she wished instead to live. For Mary Rowlandson, her ordeal seemed a test from God, one that demanded all her strength, resolution, and faith.

That first night presented a hellish scene to Mary as the natives celebrated their victory by singing, dancing, and feasting on the colonists' sheep, horses, and pigs. "All was gone (except my life)," she mourned, "and I knew not but the next moment that might go too." Separated from her other children, Mary rocked Sarah in her arms. The wounded girl moaned in pain and fever, and Mary felt helpless to ease Sarah's suffering. The next day the natives led the captives farther away from English civilization. Mary's own wound, hunger and thirst, the forced travel, the February cold, left her weak and despairing. Overcome with bitterness and sorrow, she clung to the belief that God carried her along, "bearing up my spirit, that it did not quite fail."

A

NARRATIVE

OF THE

CAPTIVITY, SUFFERINGS AND REMOVES

OF

Mrs. *Mary Rowlandson,*

Who was taken Prifoner by the INDIANS with feveral others, and treated in the moft barbarous and cruel Manner by thofe vile Savages : With many other remarkable Events during her TRAVELS.

Written by her own Hand, for her private Ufe, and now made public at the earneft Defire of fome Friends, and for the Benefit of the afflicted.

BOSTON :

Printed and Sold at JOHN BOYLE's Printing-Office, next Door to the Three Doves in Marlborough-Street. 1773.

Mary Rowlandson's *A Narrative of the Captivity, Sufferings, and Removes of Mrs. Mary Rowlandson.* Boston, 1773 edition.
Courtesy of The Rosenbach of the Free Library of Philadelphia, A773n

The Native Americans exploited Mary's fears, telling her they'd end Sarah's moaning by splitting open the girl's head. On the ninth day, February 18, Sarah died in Mary's arms. The natives buried the child, and when they moved again, leaving her daughter in the wilderness, Mary believed only "the wonderful goodness of God" kept her from taking her own life.

Around February 21 Mary knew another settlement had been attacked. She watched the victory dances and saw the display of English scalps taken as war trophies. One of the natives, with a basket of plunder, approached Mary and held out a Bible. "I was glad of it, and asked him, whether he thought the Indians would let me read? He answered, yes. So I took the Bible." This act of kindness—though not seen as such by Mary—comforted her in the weeks ahead, the Bible her "guide by day, and my pillow by night."

Mary tried to visit her daughter Mary, but the natives only let her get close enough to see the girl, but not speak with her, "which was heart-cutting," Mary wrote. "I had one child dead, another in the wilderness I knew not where, [her son, Joseph], the third they would not let me come near to."

One night Joseph appeared out of nowhere. He was held by a band of Native Americans about six miles away, and when his master left, the man's wife brought Joseph to see his mother. During her captivity Mary saw her son a few times when the boy arrived unexpectedly or she stole away to visit him. But it crushed her spirit to leave him, especially if he was sick or injured, "and no Christian friend was near him, to do any office of love for him, either for soul or body." Eventually Joseph's master sold him, and Mary didn't know if she'd ever see her son again.

Word spread through the camp that an English army approached. Mary's captors quickly packed and moved on, separating her from her daughter and from cousins and neighbors who'd shared her captivity so far. She would not see her daughter again for months. "My poor girl, I knew not where she was, nor whether she was sick, or well, or alive, or dead." Sick with worry for her children, weak from hunger, her own wound slowly healing, drained by the strain of hard travel, Mary suffered physically and mentally.

The Native Americans gave Mary little to eat. Lean times faced them all. When they came upon an English field, the natives spread out, gathering leftover ears of corn, frozen shocks of wheat, and tubers called ground nuts. The first week, Mary had hardly a bite to eat. The second week, though starving, she could barely "get down their filthy trash." But by the third week, food that before turned her stomach became "sweet and savory to my taste." She shocked herself by devouring horse liver, "with the blood about my mouth, and yet a savory bit it was to me." Another time a native woman gave her a bit of boiled horse hoof to chew. Mary ate her morsel and watched a captive English child trying to suck, gnaw, and chew the sinewy tough piece. Thinking the child too little to actually eat the horse hoof, Mary snatched the piece away and ate it herself.

In her hurry to wolf down food, Mary often burned her mouth so that it hurt for hours afterward. Sometimes she dined on only a few spoonfuls of parched wheat or a handful of acorns she found in the forest. When her master's family would not give her food, Mary wandered from dwelling to dwelling until she found "a squaw who showed herself very kind to me" and gave Mary food. Mary's mistress told her she disgraced her master by begging. They would crush her skull if she did it again. "I told them," wrote Mary, "they had as good knock me in the head as starve me to death."

At one river crossing she could not even count the numbers of Native Americans, "the enemy," that surrounded her. "They were many hundreds, old and young, some sick, and some lame; many had papooses at their backs. The greatest number at this time with us were squaws, and they traveled with all they had, bag and baggage, and yet they got over this river."

This same river halted the English army's progress even though smoke from the native's dwellings beckoned across the water. How was it, Mary wondered, desperate to be rescued, that the Native Americans "could go in great numbers over, but the English must stop." How was it that the natives, "flying for their lives" and "in such distress for food," could not be followed? How was it that even though the English destroyed fields and stashes of corn, yet the tribes found food in the wilderness and not "one man, woman, or child, die with hunger?" Mary again saw God's hand, the Native Americans his instrument, for he preserved "the heathen for further affliction to our poor country."

Mary met Metacom, whom she called Philip, several times. At their first meeting he offered her a pipe to smoke. Another time he offered her money to make a shirt and cap for his son. After that Mary bartered her useful knitting and sewing skills for food—a piece of horse or bear flesh, a quart of peas, a pancake made of parched wheat and fried in bear grease—"I thought I never tasted pleasanter meat [food] in my life," Mary recorded.

Though Mary suffered from hunger and cold, physically she seemed little abused by the Native Americans. Her writings mention being kicked, slapped, and hit; once she had ashes thrown in her eyes. She did not mention ever being raped or violated. But her captors often threatened her with violence or tormented her with tales of horror. One man told her young Joseph had been roasted, "and that himself did eat a piece of him . . . and that he was very good meat." They told Mary her husband had died or he did not want her back or he would not pay any ransom or he had already remarried in her absence. Mary comforted herself that the natives usually lied and used words to "rant and domineer."

During her captivity Mary traveled about 150 miles through Massachusetts and New Hampshire and into parts of Vermont, through forests thick with growth, rivers, and swamps, a devilish, wild environment that frightened colonists. As they traveled

Mary's hopes for "restoration" to civilization faded. She had hoped the English army would rescue her, but their attempt had failed. She had asked the natives to take her to Albany and sell her back to her husband, but the Native Americans quashed that plan. And when her native master was away, she had no hopes that any further actions would be taken. She had determined not to run away, fearing she'd be lost in the wild country. Better to leave her fate to God.

Mary's master, a chief named Quannopin, for the most part treated her well, giving her food. One time he even brought her water himself so she might wash. He had three wives and lived with each woman in turn. The wives shared Mary's labor between their households and treated her as a slave. The eldest wife, Onux, showed Mary kindness; she gave her food, a place by the fire, a mat to lie on, and a rug to cover herself.

Another wife was Wittimore or Weetamoo, who treated Mary more harshly. "A severe and proud dame," Mary labeled her, "bestowing every day in dressing herself neat as much time as any of the gentry of the land: powdering her hair, and painting her face, going with necklaces, with jewels in her ears, and bracelets upon her hands." Mary left no comment on Weetamoo as a female leader or military figure. Perhaps she didn't know Weetamoo's status, or maybe Weetamoo's behavior went too much against Mary's own ideals of Puritan womanhood.

When Weetamoo discovered Mary reading her Bible, she raged at the captive, ripped the book away, and threw it out. Mary retrieved her book but kept it out of her mistress's sight after that. Another time a servant of Philip's came to the house and asked for a piece of Mary's apron to make a flap. Mary said no. Weetamoo told her she must. Still, Mary refused. The maid said she would tear off a piece. Mary retorted she would tear the woman's coat. Weetamoo grabbed a stick, "big enough to have killed me, and struck at me with it. But I stepped out," wrote Mary, "and she struck the stick into the mat of the wigwam. But while she was pulling of it out I ran to the maid and gave her all my apron, and so that storm was over."

Weetamoo did not want to let Mary go to the eldest wife, Onux. "I understood that Weetamoo thought that if she should let me go and serve with the old squaw, she would be in danger to lose not only my service, but the redemption pay also." This thought—that the English would pay her captors money in exchange for her freedom—cheered Mary and once more raised her hopes that "an end of this sorrowful" time lay near.

Throughout her captivity Mary met with instances of kindness. Women of the tribe gave her food or a warm place by their fires. She acknowledged some of these gestures, but for the most part her captors remained Godless, bloodthirsty savages in her description. When her mistress's baby died, Mary noted, "there came a company to mourn and howl with her." Perhaps remembering Sarah's death at native hands, Mary confessed, "I could not much condole with them."

In April, two "praying" Native Americans (as Mary called those who'd converted to Christianity), Tom and Peter, arrived in camp with a letter from the Massachusetts council about the captives. Mary grasped their hands and burst into tears, asking about her husband, family, and friends. The tribe's general court gathered. Mary stood before them. What did she think her husband would give in exchange for her return? Twenty pounds, she answered. The Indians sent a message back to Boston demanding the money.

Mary's hopes rose, but then she heard news of a Native American victory at the English town of Sudbury. Meeting with Quannopin, who asked her to make clothes for his baby, she saw behind him a pile of bloody shirts, riddled with bullet holes, stripped from the English dead. "Yet the Lord suffered not this wretch to do me any hurt," she noted. Instead her master fed her "feeble carcass." As she later wrote, "So little do we prize common mercies when we have them to the full."

As usual after destroying an English town, the natives quickly moved on to escape retaliation. When several bands regrouped and built a huge wigwam to hold a day of celebration and dancing, Mary heard word that her sister and her own daughter Mary were nearby, not a mile away. She had not seen Mary in nine weeks. She had not seen her sister since their capture at the farm. Mary pleaded, begged, and persuaded, "yet so hard-hearted were they, that they would not suffer it. They made use of their tyrannical power whilst they had it; but through the Lord's wonderful mercy, their time was not but short."

On a Sunday afternoon John Hoar of Concord arrived in camp with Tom and Peter and another letter from the council. He brought Mary a pound of tobacco, sent by her husband, which she sold to the Native Americans for nine shillings. He had also sent cloth and the better part of the 20 pounds agreed upon for Mary's ransom. Mary asked the natives if she should go home with Mr. Hoar. Each of her captors answered no, and she lay down that night once more not knowing her fate. The next day and night she had the same answer. But then her master changed his mind—he would let Mary leave the next day in exchange for one pint of liquor.

Word spread, and Philip called Mary to him, asking what she would give him to let her go. Mary played along—what would Philip have? Two coats, he answered, 20 shillings, seed corn, tobacco. "I thanked him for his love; but I knew the good news as well as the crafty fox." Her master had already made a deal and had his pint of liquor.

Mary's master drank a toast to her, "showing no incivility. He was the first Indian I saw drunk all the while that I was amongst them." But still Mary could not go until the tribe's general court gave permission, which "they all as one man did seemingly consent to it, that I should go home; except Philip, who would not come among them." After three final sleepless nights "full of fears and troubles," Mary Rowlandson finally left her captivity, noting, "I was not willing to run away, but desired to wait God's time, that I might go home quietly, and without fear. And now God hath granted me my desire."

Some of the Native Americans asked her to send them things—tobacco or bread. Others shook her hand; someone gave her a scarf to wear. "So I took my leave of them, and in coming along my heart melted into tears, more than all the while I was with them, and I was almost swallowed up with the thought that ever I should go home again." When they reached Lancaster, Mary marveled, "There had I lived many comfortable years amongst my relations and neighbors, and now not one Christian to be seen, nor one house left standing."

Mary met her husband, Joseph, in Boston, their joyful reunion tempered by "thoughts of our dear children, one being dead, and the other[s] we could not tell where." Several gentlemen in Boston had raised the 20 pounds for Mary's ransom. Friends and family surrounded them. "We were in the midst of love," wrote Mary, as reports and rumors swirled about young Mary and Joseph also reaching freedom. Finally, definite word arrived that reunited the Rowlandson family. Mary rejoiced that God had given the children to her a "second time."

In the aftermath of her ordeal, sleep eluded Mary and memories tormented her. The safe haven of home and family felt elusive. She'd lived "in the midst of thousands of enemies, and nothing but death before me." Would she ever feel completely safe again?

Mary conquered her memories by facing them. She wrote the story of her capture and her life among the Native Americans. Published first in 1682, *The Narrative of the Captivity and the Restoration of Mrs. Mary Rowlandson* became an instant bestseller. She meant her book as an affirmation of her faith.

Like many Puritans, she had wished for a test from God to prove her faith, but hers came not in drops but as a sweeping rain. "Affliction I wanted, and affliction I had, full measure," she wrote. "I have seen the extreme vanity of this world: One hour I have been in health, and wealthy, wanting nothing. But the next hour in sickness and wounds, and death, having nothing but sorrow and affliction." Yet, God proved "fully able" to carry her through and, in the end, make her believe she had gained by her troubles.

4

❧⟡❧

Weary, Weary, Weary, O

---

*"Their servants they distinguish by the names of slaves
for life, and servants for a time."*
—*Robert Beverley, on the difference between
a "slave" and a "servant," 1705*

REALIZING WOMEN PROVED vital to a colony's success, each new
colony advertised abroad for single females, painting the rosiest
picture imaginable of life in the New World. In the 1634 pamphlet *New England's Prospect*, author William Wood promised
that in the colonies Englishwomen would find "as much love,
respect, and ease, as here in Old England." Wood compared an
Englishwoman's life in America to that "of these ruder *Indians*,"
hoping to assure Englishwomen they'd enjoy a life of "ease" in
comparison. Native women also compared their lot, he confided, which "hath made them miserable." Wood recommended
women even embrace the long voyage, for the sea air "purged"
weak and "foule" bodies.

Since a woman's main duty lay in marriage and childbearing, the hope of finding a husband proved a strong lure to emigrate. After all, men thickly populated the colonies compared to
the scant numbers of women. A Maryland gentleman promised
female servants "have the best luck here . . . for they are no
sooner on shoar, but they are courted into . . . Matrimony." And
from the southern colonies of North and South Carolina came
word that single women "will think themselves in the Golden
Age." As one writer promised, "If they be but civil, and under
50 years of Age, some honest Man . . . will purchase them for
their wives."

"ROOTING IN THE GROUND"

Whether they were wives or single women, female immigrants
often found the colonies had too much land, too much work,
and far too few workers. In a land of endless labor, the New
World hungered for industrious, willing hands more than anything else. Few English-born women had labored daily in the
fields back home, and those women arriving in the Chesapeake
colonies of Virginia and Maryland discovered a life far different
from the one they had left.

Here, most people grew tobacco, their chief cash crop, and
corn, the staple of their diets. By the 1630s, more than one million pounds of tobacco sailed for Europe each year. Forty years
later, 20 million pounds arrived in London warehouses, sold in
exchange for goods ordered and shipped back to colonial planters. Women might find "rooting in the ground about Tobacco
like Swine" an uncivilized way to live, but as servants or planters' wives, they probably spent hours in the fields.

Growing tobacco required backbreaking work. In spring,
workers planted long rows of seedlings by hand. Through summer's heat and humidity, they hoed weeds and battled worms
that dined on the precious crop. Fall meant long days harvesting

tobacco leaves for drying before packing them into large barrels for shipment to England. People put up with the hard work because life back in England offered few job opportunities for men or women, and even less of a chance for most people to actually own land. But they faced a life far less rosy than the one promised by colony promoters.

INDENTURED SERVANTS

Many people signed over their labor in a written contract called an indenture. They agreed to toil for a master in America for a set number of years. In exchange, the master paid for their journey to the colonies, a voyage to a life of labor and harsh conditions. More than 80 percent of immigrants to the Chesapeake in the 1600s (roughly 150,000 people) came as indentured servants. Males outnumbered females at least three to one. Once arrived, indentured servants owed their master four to seven years of work and the promise not to marry during that period.

The master, his family, and the servants usually lived together in a few crowded rooms, "the meanest Cottages in England," wrote one man in 1622, "being every ways equall (if not superior)" with the best homes in Virginia. Not until 1655 could a visitor label Virginia's homes "delightfull," if cramped. With everyone needed "to make a Cropp," the master, as well as his wife and children, often labored in the fields alongside their male and female servants.

Servants quickly bonded in a circle of companionship and mutual suffering. Sunday afternoons, the week's only free time, meant blowing off steam for both sexes with tankards of ale, pipe smoking, and gambling at cards and dice. Black men and women made up a minority of indentured servants, and in this era the races and the sexes mingled. "We and the Negroes both alike did fare," reported one servant, "of work and food we had an equal share."

"SHE DESERVES TWO OR THREE BLOWES"

Servants complained, however, of "too much worke, and too little Victuals [food]," noted master William Stephens. They bemoaned the hot sun, biting insects, loneliness, and primitive living conditions. The new climate, bouts with fevers, and exhausting drudgery felled many servants. Only half of a farm's workers might be fit for duty at any one time. After a long day's toil, many still faced hours of "beating at the mortar," grinding corn "till twelve or one o'clock" in the morning to make their own bread.

When a master or mistress gave orders, clever servants acted quickly and without complaint or question. But servants sometimes sassed back or lied, turning, as one master claimed, "more and more troublesome." They married secretly, routinely stole food and clothes, or ran away. One woman fled her master 40 times. For saucy, lazy, or otherwise ill-behaved servants, few punishments were off limits. Masters and mistresses whipped and beat servants and withheld food as common "corrections."

European indentured servants did have some rights in court. In 1649 Mistress Deborah Fernehaugh beat her maidservant Charity Dallen until the poor girl's head was "as soft as a sponge." In a rare decision, the court fined Mistress Fernehaugh and ordered Charity's indenture be sold to another master or mistress. The idea of releasing poor Charity from her indenture never occurred to anyone.

Elizabeth Sprigs, an indentured young woman in Maryland, wrote her father in London in September 1756. He'd banished the girl from his sight, for she had "offended [him] in the highest Degree" but now Elizabeth begged him to "Balance my former bad Conduct [with] my sufferings here, and then I am sure you'll pity your Destress Daughter." What she endured was beyond what anyone in England could imagine, she wrote. She toiled almost all day and night, only to be told "you Bitch you do not halfe enough, and then tied up and whipp'd to that Degree that you'd not serve an Animal." She had nothing but corn and salt to eat, and worked "almost naked no shoes nor stockings to wear." Please, she pleaded, send her some clothes by any ship heading to Baltimore. She signed off as "Your undutiful and Disobedient Child, Elizabeth Sprigs."

Some masters tried to extend the time of servitude beyond what was noted in the contract. A simple charge of "unruliness" was enough to legally tack time onto an indenture. Anne Thompson had already served six years when her master sold her indenture shortly before his death. Her new master kept Anne working for three more years, well beyond her original agreement. Anne's brother petitioned the Maryland court in 1661 for her freedom. Few servants used the courts, however, fearing worse treatment from their masters if they lost their case.

Although indenture agreements forbade servants from marrying, some female servants got pregnant. Many indentured women probably faced sexual pressures and advances from their masters and from male servants, too. Virginia lawmakers noted in 1662 "that some dissolute [immoral] masters have gotten their maides with child." In a brutal turn, time lost from work due to pregnancy and childbearing was added on to a woman's term of indenture. She owed this time, even if she'd been sexually assaulted by her master. But her extra work—two years' worth—was awarded to the parish church instead of her offending master.

A sense of desperation overcame some women. Elizabeth Greene was the sole female in a household of males in the 1660s. When Greene became pregnant she feared added years to her indenture and claimed she suffered a miscarriage. But the courts charged her with killing her baby and hanged her in 1664.

Those indentured servants who survived their ordeals hoped to build a new life in the colonies. Women shared this hope for a better future at an indenture's end and the best happily-ever-after resulted in a good marriage. "Maid servants of good honest stock," reported a Virginia planter in 1649, "may choose their husbands out of the better sort of people."

A CHANCE IN NEW ENGLAND

Compared to the Chesapeake, New England relied less on indentured servants. The area's economy didn't depend on a labor-intensive crop like tobacco, which gobbled up workers. Puritan officials also frowned on the crude and often profane behavior of many indentured servants, "both men and womenkind" who appeared too idle for Puritan tastes and too disrespectful toward Puritan faith. Besides, New Englanders preferred the labor of their own large families—sons, daughters, nieces, and nephews—to the labor of a suspicious lot of strangers. Many New England sons still worked for their fathers even after becoming adults. Daughters worked at home until they married.

Indentured servants in New England faced a better chance of charting a successful future life than their counterparts in the South. New England servants generally served less time, three to four years instead of up to seven years. More received training in craft skills or perhaps learned to read, for Puritans felt everyone should read the Bible for themselves. New England's economy grew strongly, and when a servant's indenture ended, he or she had a choice to farm, fish, trade, or keep a shop.

A SHIFT IN LABOR

In the closing decades of the 1600s, the flood of indentured servants ebbed. The economic situation in England improved, and fewer young people felt driven to leave. With fewer servants available in the colonies, those who did come could strike better terms. Newer colonies like Pennsylvania, founded in 1681, offered enticements such as shorter terms of work.

England gladly purged its shores of undesirables, unloading highwaymen, pickpockets, cutthroats, prostitutes, and Scottish and Irish rebels to the colonies. Orphans, too, were routinely shipped to America as indentured servants. But none of this quenched the need for labor in the colonies.

Colonists began looking to Africa as a reliable supply of cheap labor. A tiny number of black colonists had lived in the colonies from at least 1619. Most, like Mary and Anthony Johnson, were indentured servants who one day became free. But other black people in colonial America served as slaves, some brought from English colonies in the West Indies, like Barbados.

By the mid-1600s white legislators passed new laws that reshaped the lives of black people in the colonies. Carolina, copying the labor system in the West Indies, already depended mostly on enslaved black people for work. The Chesapeake colonies enacted the greatest changes. The Maryland General Assembly passed "An Act Concerning Negroes & Other Slaves" in September 1664. The law declared that any black person brought into the colony would now automatically serve for life. All children born to an enslaved person also became enslaved for life. Any free Englishwoman who, "to the disgrace of our Nation doe intermarry with Negro Slaves," became a slave for five years and served her husband's master.

In 1667 the Virginia Assembly examined the issue of whether or not a master must free enslaved children baptized as Christians, and decided to close this loophole to freedom. Baptizing an enslaved child, proclaimed the new law, "doth not alter the condition of the person as to his bondage or freedome." The assembly also passed various laws making it increasingly hard for masters to free a slave, fearing the evolution of a class of free black citizens.

These changing laws left many black people defenseless and trapped in bondage. Ann Joice, an indentured black woman, sailed from England to Maryland in 1668, where she worked in the kitchen of Henry Darnall. When her indenture expired,

Darnall flung Ann's indenture documents into the fire. Without her papers, and with the new laws defining slavery, Ann Joice suddenly had no legal rights to help her. To break her spirit, Darnall imprisoned Ann in a cellar for five or six months. Years later, her enslaved grandson recalled his grandmother's helpless rage: "If she had her just right that she ought to be free and all her children." The shift in law abandoned Ann Joice and her descendents to a lifetime of slavery.

The rights of free black colonists further eroded in the Chesapeake. By 1672 free black people lost their right to carry weapons. They could no longer hire white servants to work for them. By 1705 they lost their right to testify in a court of law. All legal protections had vanished.

PERPETUAL SERVITUDE

To fill the growing demand for an enslaved labor force, slave traders sailed to Africa and ripped tens of thousands of Africans from their families. They crammed the captives into ships as breathing cargo. During the filthy, suffocating voyage—called the Middle Passage—captives lay chained in rows, with as much room as a corpse in a coffin. Nearly one-fifth of the Africans died during the trip.

Survivors arrived in the colonies weak, sick, and drenched with fear. More died during their first weeks anchored in harbor as they awaited the slave auctions. They watched as buyers boarded the slave ships, these strangers speaking foreign words and wearing unfamiliar clothes. The strangers jabbed and inspected the Africans, then led them away into an alien, frightening world. The people who were not sold sailed to the next port. The process continued for about two months as the slavers made their profit.

In Africa, a young woman had been a daughter, a wife, a mother, a sister, and an aunt. In the colonies, she was connected

to no one. Homesickness, grief over the loss of her family, terror—all these ached in her bones.

Once she arrived at her new home, she listened carefully, trying to grasp words in her master's language. She learned through
observation. Do this, and no one punished you. Do that, and feel
the whip. Her master gave her a new name, or changed her African name to make it sound more English. Quickly he put her
to work in the tobacco or rice fields. She may have been used to
farming, since women farmed in many West African cultures.

One out of every four new slaves died their first year. Most
women lived on small plantations with few other black people
and often with no other African women. How could she create a new family or community as she'd known in Africa? She
lived and worked under the watch of her white owners. Her
master controlled her life. Eventually she might join with an
African man on a nearby farm, but the law recognized no marriage between slaves. The majority of women born in Africa and
taken to the colonies would have few children, maybe only one
or two, during life in slavery.

"FORBIDDEN LIBERTY"

The demand for labor grew continually, and the slave trade
expanded. Slavers sold African people as laborers all along the
Atlantic seaboard from Boston to the rice plantations of South
Carolina. The number of black people in Virginia rose from
about 300 in 1650 to about 3,000 in 1680. Between 1700 and 1740,
54,000 black people were brought to the Chesapeake as slaves.
Of those people 49,000 came directly from Africa.

White colonists needing workers viewed slavery as an economic bargain. Where indentured servants labored for a limited
time, the enslaved toiled for life. Where servants could protest
their treatment in court, slaves had no rights in court or any-
where else.

Many white people viewed Africans as non-Christian hea-
thens inferior to themselves. They believed people with dark
skin required less food, clothing, and shelter. Why waste money
providing more? A slave might die from exhaustion, but at least
no Englishman should have to spend his days "laboring in the
Corn or rice field, Broiling in the Sun, Pale and Fainting under
the Excessive heat."

Slave owners mostly wanted the physical strength of male
workers, but a woman had value, too. Her children automatically belonged to her master, increasing his number of slaves
without spending further money. "It is therefore advantageous
to have Negro women," a Swedish visitor explained. Sometimes
the master himself impregnated a female slave, increasing his
slave holdings with one of his own children.

A healthy black woman almost always worked in the fields.
As more black women cultivated, harvested, and carried crops,

An Overseer Doing His Duty Near Fredericksburg, Virginia, watercolor sketch
by Benjamin Latrobe, 1793.
Courtesy of the Maryland Historical Society, item ID# 1960.108.1.3.21

fewer white women were needed in the fields. "Sufficient Distinction is also made between the Female-Servants, and Slaves" wrote Robert Beverley in the early 1700s, "for a White Woman is rarely or never put to work in the Ground, if she be good for anything else."

Most slaveholders, especially in the North, owned only a few slaves, and fewer slaves lived in the North overall. Northern slaves worked in less brutal conditions and performed a wider range of jobs. An enslaved woman might cook, clean, spin thread, milk cows, raise poultry, or watch her master's children. Slaves in cities such as Philadelphia and New York organized churches and formed communities with other enslaved black people.

Solidarity among the enslaved, however, made white colonists uneasy. The slaves' "continual aspiring after their forbidden Liberty, renders them Unwilling servants," noted Massachusetts judge Samuel Sewall in 1700. The enslaved fought back daily in quiet ways. Masters complained of slaves stealing, sabotaging work, feigning illness, and of work slowdowns, described as laziness.

Slave uprisings were rare, but violent. Black women as well as men were arrested in an uprising in New York in 1712. The Stono Rebellion in South Carolina shocked the white population. In September 1739, 20 black Carolinians seized guns and gunpowder from a local store. Their ranks swelled to more than 100 as the rebels headed south, burning houses and killing white people who tried to stop them. By the time the revolt ended, 20 white people and 40 black people lay dead. Even with rage seething beneath the system, slavery grew more deeply entrenched in the colonies.

Elizabeth Ashbridge
From Indentured Servant to Quaker Preacher

WHEN 14-YEAR-OLD ELIZABETH Sampson (later, Elizabeth Ashbridge) surrendered to a "foolish passion," she set herself upon a path of "sorrows." Born in 1713 in Middlewich, England, Elizabeth rarely saw her father, a ship's surgeon often away on lengthy voyages. Her mother instilled in her daughter "the principles of virtue" found in the Anglican church, officially called the Church of England. Young Elizabeth felt awed by religion and churchmen and wished she too might be "beloved of God." Troubled, Elizabeth observed there were different religious groups. Which was the true religion? She prayed God would point the way for her.

Instead, God pointed Elizabeth toward love. She tumbled into her "foolish passion" and under a blanket of night, secretly eloped with a young stocking weaver. Her elopement flaunted her parents' right to dispose of Elizabeth in marriage with a man of their choice. At the very least, according to the practice of the day, Elizabeth should have consulted her parents in the matter.

Guilt over her disobedience haunted the girl. Five months later, when death stripped Elizabeth "of the darling of my heart," widowhood seemed to her a fitting punishment for her rash behavior. Her father shunned his homeless daughter, and Elizabeth's mother, helpless to act against her husband's wishes, eventually sent the girl to a relative near Dublin, Ireland, hoping her husband would soften. But Elizabeth's father did not send for her; without his permission, she could not return home.

Elizabeth spent more than three years in Ireland, first at the house of a Quaker relation who forbid the vivacious teenager to sing or dance. Elizabeth rebelled under this strictness and grew "more wild and airy than ever." The Quaker packed her off to another relation, who let the girl do just as she pleased. But this freedom rang hollow. Still rejected by her father, Elizabeth sought religious answers. She befriended a Catholic woman who nearly converted Elizabeth to the faith. But as the girl pondered the tenets of "the popish church" Elizabeth once again plunged without thought into a life-changing decision.

Elizabeth's mother had a brother living across the sea in Pennsylvania. A woman visiting from that American colony talked Elizabeth into returning with her. It must have seemed like a romantic adventure for a girl disowned by her father. "I soon agreed with her [the woman] for my passage," wrote Elizabeth, "& being ignorant of the nature of an indenture," she did not realize she'd bound herself as a servant to the woman in exchange for her travel.

Once onboard the ship, Elizabeth discovered she'd been tricked, and when she tried to go ashore, her way was blocked. For three weeks, she remained captive on the ship and was only released when friends of another deceived girl discovered her whereabouts. Undaunted by her near escape from servitude, Elizabeth wrote, "I was so filled with the thoughts of going to America that I could not give up the design."

With no word of acceptance from her father, Elizabeth determined again to try America—"since my Absence was so Agreeable, he should have it." She returned to the vessel; "meeting the
captain, I inquired when he sailed; he told me, and I went on
board." The ship's passengers included 60 Irish servants and several English travelers. Twenty of the servants belonged to the
Pennsylvania woman who'd first recruited Elizabeth. It seems
Elizabeth no longer felt herself tied to any indenture agreement,
a naïve and probably even foolish belief on her part.

For several weeks the wind held the ship at bay along the
coast of Ireland, and one night Elizabeth overheard a plot by
some of the servants. They planned to gain their freedom in
America by killing the ship's crew and English passengers and
seizing the vessel.

Elizabeth reported the plot to the captain. The next day he
invited people to enjoy time ashore before they left Ireland. Once
the conspirators disembarked, the captain ordered his men to
weigh anchor and hoist sails, leaving them behind. Nine weeks
later, in July 1732, the ship arrived in New York. Here Elizabeth's
good deed ended in betrayal when the captain, whose life and
ship she had saved, penned an indenture paper and threatened
her with jail if she didn't sign it. It appears Elizabeth had not paid
for her passage. The captain probably assumed he'd get paid by
selling her into servitude.

Elizabeth offered to find funds to pay for her passage without
becoming bound, but the captain offered her only two choices:
sign his indenture or he'd enforce the one she'd already signed
in Ireland. Knowing the woman who'd recruited her in Ireland
"was a vile creature," the frightened girl signed the captain's
indenture papers. Two weeks later he sold her into servitude. "I
was a Stranger in a Strange Land," Elizabeth wrote.

At first Elizabeth's life seemed tolerable. But then "a Difference that happened between my Master & Me, wherein I was
Innocent" turned her life to misery. Elizabeth had probably

fended off her master's sexual advances, or perhaps become a victim, a common occurrence in the life of indentured young women. She suffered "the Utmost Hardship that my Body was able to Bear," harsh drudgery, lack of food and decent clothing, no shoes to wear in the winter snow. All the while, her cruel master prayed nightly with his family, and Elizabeth wondered if God heard prayers from such "polluted lips." Sunk in her own miseries, "I became hardened, and was ready to conclude that there was no God."

Two years after the event, Elizabeth confessed to another woman the nature of the "difference" with her master. When he learned about her confession, he sent for "the Town Whipper to Correct [her]." Her master ordered her to strip. Elizabeth pleaded with her master, reminding him he knew the truth and that she, unlike him, had kept her principles and not "told it before his wife." She begged him to spare her shame, before finishing, "if you think I deserve such punishment, do it yourself." The man stalked around the room and then sent the whipper away.

Elizabeth had saved herself a whipping, but afterward "suffered so much cruelty that I could not bear it; and was tempted to put an end to my miserable life." At one point she tried to hang herself. But in that dark moment Elizabeth heard a voice say, "There is a hell beyond the grave," and she cried for mercy and strength to bear her sufferings. Days later she dreamed of a woman holding a lamp who said if Elizabeth returned to the Lord, he would have mercy on her. But Elizabeth wasn't ready to embrace religion, which had seemed to abandon her.

A talented and passionate singer and dancer, Elizabeth fell in with a company of play actors who invited her to join them. Though pleased with the proposal, she declined, worried what her father would think. He had finally asked to see his daughter again. Elizabeth, however, had too much pride to return home as an abused servant, showing her parent the proof and punishment for her disobedience to him. After serving her master nearly three years, she bought off the rest of her indenture contract and found lucrative work as a seamstress. But her independence didn't last long; she "was not Sufficiently Punished."

> I released myself from one cruel Servitude & then not Contented got into another, and this for Life. A few months after, I married a young man that fell in Love with me for my Dancing, a Poor Motive for a man to Choose a Wife, or a Woman a Husband. But for my Part, I fell in Love with nothing I saw in him.

Her new husband, a schoolmaster named Sullivan, like Elizabeth, had no religion, and when drunk the man swore such oaths that burned her ears.

At age 22 Elizabeth determined she must rescue her own life. As she had in childhood, Elizabeth sought people of different religious societies, including Baptists, Presbyterians, and Catholics, while still attending Church of England services. She resolved to find the truth that might lead her to God. "My husband did not oppose me, for he saw I grew more affectionate to him; and as yet, I did not refuse to sing and dance, when he asked me."

In Boston Elizabeth attended a Quaker meeting. Since the sect's founding by George Fox in the mid-16th century, the Quakers, or Society of Friends, had faced abuse and hatred for their distinctive beliefs. They refused to attend mandatory Anglican services and would not pay church tithes. They renounced war and weapons. They spurned taking oaths and doffing their hats to their betters.

Quakers believed an "inner light" guided people toward divine truth. Members often sat in their meetings in silence waiting for divine inspiration to speak. Unlike other religions, which excluded women from active participation, Quakers believed males and females enjoyed equality in the eyes of God.

But Elizabeth found no solace in the Quaker silence or their words and felt nothing but shock and contempt when a woman rose to preach.

Elizabeth and her husband moved around New York and New England as his teaching jobs led them, usually renting a room in a house. Elizabeth felt unloved by God, engulfed in sin—at one point she horrified herself by stealing a bunch of flax, which she quickly returned. Despair robbed her of sleep, her appetite, and her delight in the world around her. "Had all the world been mine, I would have given it gladly for one glimpse of hope," she wrote. Her change shocked her husband, and she noted, "my singing was turned into mourning, and my dancing into lamentation." Again, she contemplated taking her own life.

Her husband allowed Elizabeth to visit relatives in Pennsylvania. She almost turned back upon learning they were Quakers

A Quaker woman preaching. *Public domain*

and, "what was worse of all, that my aunt was a preacher." Elizabeth's relatives treated her with kindness. She listened to their
manner of speech using *thee, thou,* and *thy.* One day, she took a
short Quaker book to read and felt immediately struck by the
teachings. Reduced to tears, she wondered if she'd found her
spiritual home at last. But the next day, at church with her relatives, her old questions began. "As we sat in silence, I looked
over the meeting, and said to myself, 'How like fools these people sit; how much better would it be to stay at home, and read
the Bible, . . . than come here and go to sleep.'"

Within weeks Elizabeth moved from despising the Quakers to realizing that for her, the Friends offered the true path.
At an afternoon meeting at her uncle's house, she heard William Hammans preach the gospel "with such power that I was
obliged to confess it was the truth." Surprised, Elizabeth real-
ized that all she'd gone through—her suffering, her doubts, her
feelings of unworthiness—had prepared her for this day.

But she feared openly acknowledging her Quakerism. She
began teaching school and sent for her husband to join her. She
would sneak from school through the woods to attend meetings. Neighbors began to revile her, calling her a fool and asking if she'd soon turn preacher. In order to hide her true opinions Elizabeth dressed in fancier gowns than the plain dress of
Quaker women.

But Elizabeth's husband had heard she'd turned Quaker.
When, after a four-month separation she greeted him, "My
dear, I am glad to see thee," he flew into a rage: "The devil thee,
thee thee, don't thee me."

Even when they moved away from her Quaker relatives Elizabeth felt her husband's disapproval, and this strained an already
unhappy the marriage. He told her if she ever turned preacher,
"You had better be hanged in that day." "I was seized with horror," Elizabeth recalled, "and again plunged into despair. . . . I
was afraid that, by denying the Lord, the heavens would be shut

against me." Sunk into a depression that lasted three months, she ate little and wandered the woods, seeking guidance.

Elizabeth's husband hoped to cure her of her new religion. But Elizabeth found the strength to stand up to him. As a dutiful wife, she'd obey all his lawful commands, but when it came to her own conscience, she could not obey him. "I had already wronged myself," she wrote, "in having done it too long."

When her husband forbade Elizabeth to gather with the Quakers, she went anyway, walking eight miles to the meetinghouse. He beat her for such disobedience and one night threatened her with a knife, claiming he would cripple her if she set off for the meetinghouse, "for you shall not be a Quaker."

Elizabeth prayed. She appealed to her husband. Would she have struggled so if she didn't feel it her duty, she asked him. Eventually the man relented, deciding if her conversion "be of God I cannot overthrow it; and, if of yourself, it will soon fall." One day he even agreed to attend church with her, "only I'm afraid I shall hear you clack [preach], which I cannot bear," he told her. If Elizabeth rose to speak at the meetings, her husband left.

But their truce failed. Her husband began drinking heavily, and when drunk, he turned violent. In 1740, in a "drunken frolic," he deserted her, enlisted in the army, and months later died in a hospital near London back in England.

After Sullivan's death, Elizabeth supported herself as a schoolteacher and seamstress. Once horrified that a woman might preach, by age 27 she was an active preacher for the Quakers, who believed God chose a select few, both male and female, to spread His word. Elizabeth also served as the clerk for the women's monthly meetings.

In May 1746 she wed a fellow Quaker, Aaron Ashbridge, and finally entered a satisfying and fulfilling time of her life. Elizabeth spoke at Quaker meetings including Philadelphia's General Spring Meeting of ministers and elders in March 1752. The

event's roster is the only surviving document bearing her signa-
ture. In 1753 Elizabeth was recorded as a minister of the church
and later spoke throughout England and Ireland. She died in
Ireland on May 16, 1755, the end of her spiritual journey that
began with a girl shunned by her father, sold into servitude, and
at last reaching the far side of a black depression to find the place
she fit best.

5

⊰❧❧⊱

Up to Their Elbows in Housewifery

Pease porridge hot,
Pease porridge cold,
Pease porridge in the pot,
Nine days old!

—*from an old English nursery rhyme*

SHE ROSE AT DAWN, wearing her shift, and over that she donned stiffened stays—later known as a corset. She drew on her petticoat and over that slid into her gown, a skirt and bodice joined together. The wealthy wore silk, the poor a rougher linen or wool. The gown opened in the front to reveal her petticoat, some worked with embroidery or quilted for warmth. An apron protected her clothes, and a cap covered her hair. A woman of wealth might also wear a petticoat shaped by wooden hoops that lifted her gown out fashionably over the hip. Clothes marked

Tight Lacing, or Fashion Before Ease, engraving published in London around 1770. *The Colonial Williamsburg Foundation, Museum Purchase*

a woman's place in society; finery and tight lacing of her stays showed she had servants or slaves to do her bidding.

Wherever she lived, whether in a colonial town, on a farm, or on the distant frontier, she began her days with a dizzying whirl of daily chores. Her family's survival often depended upon her skills and efforts—her mastering of housewifery.

KEEPING THE KETTLE FILLED

The house and yard, including the dairy barn, kitchen garden, pigsty, and henhouse, served as the workplace for most colonial women. Preparing food consumed much of a woman's day. In the gray morning chill, she reached beneath her hens and gathered fresh-laid eggs. She crouched on a milking stool next to her cow and listened to the rhythmic hiss of warm milk ricocheting into her pail. She picked an apron full of vegetables and herbs from her kitchen garden, then hurried inside to begin breakfast. She might fry some cornmeal or slice bread and serve it with butter or leftover cold meat.

Dinner, served at midday, was the largest meal. Many women cooked a pottage—a simple one-pot meal of meat or fish boiled with cabbage, beans, and other vegetables. Families rounded out the meal with cheese and bread, washed down with a hearty mug of home-brewed beer or cider. Depending on the season she might serve a special dish of roast pork or an eel pie. Most people made the evening's supper a frugal meal—a slice of bread and a cup of milk. In hard times the poor might skip supper altogether.

A 1684 engraving shows
different cooking skills.
Library of Congress,
LC-USZ62-78099

Poorer families lived mostly on baked and boiled cornmeal flavored with a bit of salted beef or bacon. Wealthier women could provide a sumptuous spread cooked and served by servants. A visitor to a prosperous Virginian's home described "tables fournished with porke, kidd [young goat], chickens, turkeys, young geese . . . besides plentie of milk, cheese, butter, and corn."

Kitchen work required muscle. Women churned cream into butter. They squeezed whey from cheese. They lifted heavy iron pots and skillets. A wooden bucket filled with water and hauled from a well or spring weighed about 20 pounds.

Cooking meant standing on the hearth of a large fireplace—even in summer's heat—with her skirts tucked up for safety. Temperatures on the hearth reached about 170 degrees, and many women suffered burns and scalding. Some burned to death when their clothing caught fire. A woman prepared meals over several fires at a time and also set pots over mounds

Colonial kitchen with cooking fireplace and hearth.
Brandon Marie Miller at Colonial Williamsburg

The Art of Dressing Fish, engraving, 1773.
The Colonial Williamsburg Foundation, Museum Purchase

of red-hot coals on her hearth. She determined just when the brick oven was hot enough for baking bread by thrusting her arm inside the oven, then counting how long she could stand the heat.

Cooking also required a basic knowledge of chemical reactions. A woman knew how to turn yeast cultures, water, and flour into bread. Her labor transformed milk and rennet (from a calf's stomach) into cheese. In October she brewed malt, herbs, and hops into beer and made watered-down small beer several times a month. She preserved fruit from her orchard into jugs of ciders—the "singing of the cider," the sounds as mashed apples fermented, bubbled, and hissed, was another song for autumn. From her slaughtered pigs she ground, seasoned, and stuffed sausages, and she pickled and smoked cuts of meat.

Always, she kept an eye toward stocking her cellar and loft with supplies for winter, when fresh food grew scarce. When Beatrice Plummer's husband died in 1672, the Newbury, Massachusetts, court inventoried his farm. The list included provisions Beatrice had squirreled away for winter. She'd salted and smoked four and a half sides of bacon. She'd turned pails of milk into 28 pounds of cheese and four pounds of butter. She'd gathered 25 bushels of grain (barley, oats, wheat, and rye) for future baking and brewing. She'd harvested and dried bushels of peas and beans. She'd brewed a barrel of cider. She'd grown and harvested cabbages and turnips by the sackful. Beatrice had also purchased, or traded for, quantities of sugar, spices, and molasses.

One 17th-century New England woman claimed that a wife "utterly ignorant" in food skills could only perform half her marriage vow. "She may love and obey," wrote the woman, "but she cannot cherish, serve, and keep him with that true duty which is ever expected."

"NO SOONER COME, BUT GONE"

A woman guarded her family's health and nursed the sick, armed with minerals (such as iron), herbs, tree barks, even sheep's dung. She worked her cures through homemade potions and steeped teas. People of the day believed the worst-tasting medicines worked the best. She soaked squares of flannel or linen in medicines and laid these plasters upon the skin to raise blisters so disease might escape. She prepared poultices, or pastes, to relieve pain and swelling and to reduce pus.

Without refrigeration, food spoiled, and people suffered a host of stomach ailments. No one knew bacteria and viruses caused and spread disease, and there was little anyone could do to treat epidemics of smallpox, measles, diphtheria, influenza, malaria, and pneumonia, diseases that swept through colonial villages and towns, decimating the population.

Rachel Weeping, artist Charles Willson Peale's portrait of his wife with the body of their daughter, Margaret, who died of smallpox in 1772. He added Rachel to the portrait in 1776.
Courtesy of the Philadelphia Museum of Art, Rachel Weeping, *by Charles Willson Peale*

Medical treatments relied heavily on opening a vein and allowing patients to bleed into a bowl. Other cures included purges both "upward" and "downward." In the 1720s an inoculation to prevent smallpox was introduced with some success. Many colonists, however, remained suspicious of the procedure since it involved scooping pus from an infected person and scratching it into the skin of a healthy person.

Few colonial households escaped the haunting presence of death. Next to smallpox, diphtheria (sometimes called "putrid throat disease") stalked families as the colonies' greatest killer. Many mothers buried children before their fifth birthday. Many more children died before they reached adulthood. Anne Bradstreet wrote a poem in 1669 on the death of her one-month-old grandson, Simon, beginning with sad words echoed by many parents: "No sooner come, but gone."

SHIRTS AND SHIFTS

Making clothes posed another time-consuming task for colonial women. Sometimes the process started from scratch, with shearing the sheep's wool. Following the shearing, a woman washed, carded, and combed the wool. Then she spun it out into thread, dipped the skeins into homemade dyes, and wove the threads into fabric on her loom. From sheep shearing to sewn shirt required nearly a year of work. Many women could not afford their own spinning wheel or loom. They traded goods or labor for the fabric needed to sew clothes—or paid with precious cash, if they were lucky enough to have any.

To make linen, a colonial woman cut flax plants, soaked and dried them, then pounded the stalks to break down the tough plant fibers. Then the fibers were spun, dyed, and woven into linen. Women used linen to sew shirts and shifts—underclothes—as well as aprons, caps, and baby dresses. Luxuries like tablecloths, napkins, and sheets were also sewn from linen.

A more well-off woman hired a tailor or dressmaker to sew fitted dress tops (bodices), jackets, and men's breeches. Wealthier women ordered material from England. Many southern women ordered fabric from English stores when the tobacco crop shipped for sale. Nearly all women handled a needle, thread, and thimble with skill. Clothing required yards and yards of fabric, and each tiny stitch on every garment was sewn by hand. Sewing, mending, or altering a family's clothes proved a constant chore. Women also knitted stockings and caps.

Since clothes were expensive and time-consuming to make, most colonists possessed scant wardrobes. Only the wealthy could afford lace, fancy buttons, or embroidery silks that set their clothes above the common folk. Sumptuary laws actually decreed that a craftsman's wife or a poor farm woman must not dress like her betters.

A woman also counted laundry among her chores, washing the family's linens (about once a month) and infants' diapers. She scrubbed clothes stooped over a washtub filled with water she'd lugged from well or stream and heated over a fire. After wringing each piece by hand, she hung the clothes to dry in the summer breeze or freeze-dry in the winter cold.

Clothes made from wool, or expensive fabrics like silks, were not washed for fear they'd be ruined. Women spot cleaned these garments, brushed away dust and dirt, aired them out, and stored the clothes in chests with dried herbs. Dirty garments and seldom-washed bodies did not make for sweet-smelling colonists.

HELPING HANDS

Whenever possible, women enlivened their drudgery by sharing. They organized cornhusking and quilting parties. They competed to see who'd pick the most berries, spin the most thread, or dip the most candles. Gossip and refreshments fueled the labor.

Many women saved work by bartering goods and services. A thriving trade network flourished: Goodwife Smith swapped candles she'd dipped or a crock of churned butter for a batch of soap boiled up by Goodwife Jones. Women enlisted their daughters for help with housekeeping, at the same time providing hands-on training in the skills girls would need as adults. William Byrd II, a wealthy Virginian, wrote about his daughters in 1727: "They are every day up to their Elbows in Housewifery, which will qualify them . . . for useful Wives and if they live long enough, for Notable Women."

Women living on small farms or on the frontier continued working in the fields as well as tending to household jobs. All women juggled chores while managing the needs of infants, toddlers, and children. Many complained that their lives possessed a weary "sameness . . . throughout the year."

While a busy, frugal woman earned a shining reputation, disgrace marked an idle housewife. No wonder Anne Bradstreet's brother-in-law assured readers Anne hadn't neglected her duties to loll about scribbling poems. "These poems are the fruit but of some few houres," he claimed, "curtailed from her sleep and other refreshments."

EARNING HER KEEP

Colonial women earned income or goods in a variety of ways. If a town wife helped run the family shop, she paid wages to other women to wash clothes or cook. She could spend less time growing vegetables; instead she bought food carted to town by farm wives or servants. Many young women worked as servants in the households of wealthier colonists. Colonial families were often large, and sending a daughter to live, eat, and work with another family saved money.

As an extension of their role as housewives, women— especially widows—took in boarders or ran taverns and inns.

Taverns hummed as noisy gathering spots, sources of news and juicy gossip. An innkeeper and her staff served food and drink, provided lodgings, and managed a local lost and found. One enterprising woman capitalized on her strategic location at a river crossing in Maryland. In 1657 Mrs. Fenwick earned 500 pounds of tobacco for "her trouble and charge in entertaining and setting people over the river." Another female innkeeper enticed customers to a 1738 dance at her establishment by offering a raffle prize: "A Virginia Negro woman fit for house business and her child."

Women transformed other housewifery skills into income. Lydia Dyar advertised flower and vegetable seeds for sale in the *Boston Evening Post*. Mary Crathorne ran advertisements in the *Pennsylvania Gazette* announcing she sold bottled mustards, raisins, and pickles. Women earned as dressmakers, hatmakers, spinners, and weavers. They washed clothes and starched laces. They sold fine needlework as bed hangings and cushions. Sister Bradish baked and brewed for Harvard students in the 1650s and comforted the homesick. A woman known only as Mistress Hewlett of Ipswich ran a poultry business and loaned her husband money. Legally, all her earnings belonged to him, but Mr. Hewlett commented, "I meddle not with the geese nor the turkeys For they are hers for she has been and is a good wife to me."

Some women earned cash or goods as midwives and nurses. Elizabeth Girardeau of South Carolina advertised she would take in persons recovering from smallpox inoculations, "where the best attendance will be given at Ten pounds per week." Women advertised homemade remedies for sale, claiming cures for everything from eye ailments to purging children infested with worms.

And women with housewifery skills remained, as they had since the early days at Jamestown, a steadying influence on men. When James Oglethorpe founded Georgia in 1733, the last of the 13 colonies, he advertised seeking wives for his soldiers. Married soldiers, he noted, proved the most industrious and willing to plant roots in American soil.

MARGARET BRENT

Margaret Brent, an English Catholic, arrived in Maryland in 1638. She came as an unmarried woman in her late 30s with a sister and two brothers. Highly unusual for the time, Margaret remained unmarried and controlled her own landholdings and business affairs as a tobacco planter. She sued in court and collected debts and often acted as an agent for her brothers.

In 1645 the civil war raging in England between the Puritan Protestants who controlled Parliament and King Charles I spread to Maryland. A rampaging army of Protestants destroyed the property of Maryland Catholics. The governor, Leonard Calvert, a member of the Catholic Calvert clan that had founded Maryland, fled to Virginia. He returned to Maryland at the head of his own army to regain control of the colony. But he died in 1647 with Maryland's fate and his own personal affairs still in crisis. On his deathbed, Calvert appointed Margaret Brent his executor. He trusted Margaret, but he'd left her a nearly impossible task.

Margaret had to pay Calvert's debts, including wages for the soldiers he'd hired. Unpaid for six months, they stood on the brink of mutiny. Margaret asked the Maryland Assembly to grant her emergency powers—give her Leonard Calvert's power of attorney for his brother, Lord Baltimore, who lived in England. With the situation dire, the assembly agreed, and Margaret sold Lord Baltimore's cattle to pay the troops and avert disaster, saving the colony but angering the powerful Lord Baltimore.

But Mistress Brent did one more thing: in January 1648 she boldly asked the Maryland legislature to grant her two votes in the assembly, one for herself and one as Lord Baltimore's representative. The legislators would not go this far, for no woman was allowed to vote in the assembly. Her request quickly squashed, "the said Mistress Brent protested against all proceedings in this present Assembly, unless she may be present and vote."

The assembly, trying to smooth matters over with Lord Baltimore, paid Margaret tribute, however, in a letter to the Englishman, recognizing her courage and skill.

We do Verily Believe and in Conscience report that it was better for the Colonies safety at that time in her hands then in any mans else in the whole Province after your Brothers death for the Soldiers would never have treated any other with the Civility and respect and though they were even ready at times to run into mutiny yet she still pacified them till at the last things were brought to that strait that she must be admitted and declared your Lordships Attorney . . . or else all must go to ruin again . . . . We conceive from that time she rather deserved favor and thanks from your Honor for her so much Concurring to the public safety then to be justly liable to all those bitter invectives you have been pleased to Express against her.

His Lordship remained unsoothed and incensed that Margaret had sold his cattle. Out of favor with the powerful Lord Baltimore, Margaret moved to Virginia in 1651, where she lived until her death around 1671.

"SHE MERCHANTS"

A handful of women, like Margaret Brent, ran businesses in their own right. Margaret Hardenbroeck settled in New Amsterdam in 1659 and ran a successful shipping and trade business. She

The Rival Milleners, 1772. Two female business owners vie for a customer.
The Colonial Williamsburg Foundation, Museum Purchase

was one of 134 women involved in business in the Dutch colony.
After the English takeover in 1664, new laws forbade Margaret
from owning property or purchasing goods in her own name,
granting that power to her husband. By the time of Margaret's death in 1691, the number of women business owners had
shrunk dramatically—down to 43 female proprietors.

For other women, a husband's death propelled them into the
business world. Widows often continued running their departed
husbands' businesses—even in traditionally male jobs like
blacksmith, tanner, and shipwright. Upon her husband's death
in 1738, Elizabeth Timothy took over publishing the *South Carolina Gazette.* She hoped her subscribers "will be kindly pleased to
continue their Favours . . . to his poor afflicted Widow with six
small Children and another hourly expected."

In January 1733 a revolutionary spirit stirred the widowed
businesswomen of New York. "We are House Keepers, Pay our

Taxes, carry on Trade, and most of us are She Merchants," they explained in the *New York Journal*, "and as we in some measure contribute to the Support of Government, we ought to be Intitled to some of the Sweets of it; but we find ourselves entirely neglected."

Like male businessmen, women often petitioned the courts to help collect what customers owed. As shop owner Agnes Lind advertised in February 1765, "all persons indebted to her are desired to pay off their accounts, especially those of two or three years standing, otherwise they may expect to find them in the hands of an attorney at law."

But most colonial women did not venture deeply into the business world. They remained fixed in their sphere of house and hearth. At best, many possessed a mere smattering of education. Only about 30 percent could read or write, about half the percentage of literate men. In general, people viewed education as dangerous to women, whose minds many believed couldn't withstand the rigor of study. John Winthrop related the sad case of Mrs. Hopkins who had fallen

> into a sad infirmity, the loss of her understanding and reason . . . by occasion of her giving herself wholly to reading and writing, and had written many books. For if she had attended her household affairs, and such things as belong to women, and not gone out of her way . . . to meddle in such things as are proper for men, whose minds are stronger, she [might] had kept her wits, and might have improved them usefully and honorably.

Margaret Hardenbroeck Philipse
She-Merchant of New York

AFTER TWO MONTHS AT sea, 22-year-old Margaret Hardenbroeck arrived in Manhattan, the port city for the Dutch colony of New Amsterdam. She made the 1659 trip alone, without the protection of her father, one of her brothers, or even an uncle. This North American outpost, with its fort and tiny shipyard and warehouses, was a far cry from bustling old Amsterdam, but like any city in the Netherlands, this place too promised the excitement of trade and money to be made. And that's what concerned Margaret Hardenbroeck, for she'd arrived in New Amsterdam as a businesswoman.

Margaret stepped off the boat as a factor, a representative of her cousin, a Dutch merchant. She would collect money owed him, seek new buyers for the goods he shipped, and pen detailed reports of her progress on his behalf. She could also represent his affairs, if necessary, in court, where suing and being sued played a large role in the busy world of Dutch trading.

Born to a trading family in 1637, Margaret had the good fortune to grow up in the Netherlands. This tiny republic, amid all

122

New Amsterdam, around 1660. *US History Images*

of Europe's monarchies, offered women the basic rights and protections that men enjoyed. Laws entitled Margaret to the same
elementary education as any boy—the only 17th-century European country offering this advantage to girls. And women of
business—she-merchants—were a respected and *expected* sight
in Holland. A court document from 1664 recorded Margaret's
status among that rank as a "free agent of New Amsterdam."

The tiny outpost of New Amsterdam offered Dutch traders a
wondrous horde of goods clamored after in Europe. Foremost,
traders sought animal hides and fur pelts. Native American
hunters exchanged thousands of furs for rum, guns, and bolts
of Dutch cloth. Belts of strung shell beads, known as wampum,
served as money. Other hot commodities included the giant
logs (long depleted in Europe) so necessary for shipbuilding and
crumbled tobacco for the white clay pipes that everyone, even
women, smoked.

Within months of her arrival, Margaret married a prosperous trader named Pieter Rudolphus de Vries, a 56-year-old widower she may have known back in Amsterdam. She continued working for her cousin while the couple built their own import-export business, heavy on tobacco. They owned one ship and five properties around Manhattan. The vessel sailed, crammed with goods packed in hogshead barrels branded with Margaret's initials, MH.

In May 1660, the couple welcomed a daughter they named Maria. But within a year, Pieter died, leaving Margaret a young widow with their family business to run. Margaret sold some of her real estate and bought two more ships, setting herself up as an independent wholesale merchant. Again, she benefited from Dutch law regarding wives and widows.

A Dutch wife could choose to enter marriage with an arrangement, called *manus*. This was similar to English law, which placed a woman, like a child, under the guidance of her husband. Legally, she could not enter into contracts, bring lawsuits, or make decisions about her own property. Everything she had belonged to her spouse. In the Netherlands a widow was entitled to half her husband's estate, different from English law, which awarded a widow use of only one-third of her husband's estate. In Holland, children could be treated equally in a father's will, whereas English law used sex and birth order to determine inheritance—the eldest son inherited the bulk of his father's estate while daughters received mainly household goods.

But a Dutch woman had another choice. And when Margaret married her second husband, Frederick Philipse, in 1662, she opted for *usus*, a prenuptial agreement that granted her the same and equal rights she enjoyed as a single woman. Husband and wife became equal partners. Margaret could continue appearing in court, or she could represent her husband in court. She could make contracts and conduct business. Most important, her ships, her fine linens, her plate (utensils, dishes, platters, and such), her house lots—everything remained her own. And she had several years of court wrangling ahead defending Pieter's estate.

Margaret entered the marriage as the wealthier spouse by far. Frederick worked as a master carpenter, and like many artisans of New Netherland, he'd embraced trading. Frederick adopted two-and-a-half-year-old Maria, declaring he'd make her an heir, joint and equal, with his own children. He changed her name to Eva Philipse. If love was a consideration of the marriage, business was the bedrock it rested on, as year by year Margaret and Frederick built a commercial empire.

Margaret ran her businesses, oversaw the Philipse household, and added four more children to the family: Philip, Adolph, another daughter named Annetje, and a last son called Rombout who probably died in childhood. The couple built a bigger house and added ships to their fleet of trade vessels.

In 1664 a tremendous change swept through New Amsterdam. An English fleet sailed into the harbor, intent on taking over this Dutch possession stuck in the middle of England's own North American colonies. Outmanned and outgunned, New Amsterdam surrendered to the English two weeks later without a shot fired. Male inhabitants swore an oath of allegiance to the English king, Charles II. Overnight, New Amsterdam became New York, named for the king's brother, James, Duke of York.

At first the English made only small changes, and during this time Margaret and Frederick moved to expand their businesses. They received permission to deal directly with Native Americans around Albany, the center of the fur trade, which turned them into major players in that lucrative business. They also stashed huge supplies of wampum and made a fortune when the value of the strung shells rose 400 percent after the English takeover.

But over time, England placed more restrictions on Dutch merchants who competed so successfully with England's own trade. They hit Dutch vessels with higher taxes and limited the number of foreign vessels (Dutch) that could carry goods to and from North America to three a year. When that number was suddenly lowered to one, Margaret, on a 1668 business trip to Amsterdam, was caught with a shipload of goods stuck in the harbor.

Margaret responded by boldly writing to the English king— "Your sacred Majesty"—pleading for an exception as the rule would leave her in a "ruinous condition." On December 11, 1668, the king granted Margaret special permission to sail.

Over the years, English rule not only restricted Dutch trading and shipping but eroded the long-standing rights enjoyed by Margaret and other Dutch women. Eventually, Margaret could no longer own property in her name, sign contracts, or represent herself in court. Her public role as a free she-merchant vanished. English law forced her to work through Frederick or shift business practices away from the watchful gaze of English authorities. When Frederick was listed as the richest man in New York in 1675, there was no measure or mention of Margaret's wealth or status, for that had ceased to exist outside the shadow of her husband.

The couple stayed as busy as ever. They began purchasing land with easy access to the Hudson River above Manhattan. There, Margaret built a large house in keeping with the family's status. Though not luxurious by later standards, the home built of brick and sparkling gray granite boasted a fireplace surrounded by Dutch tiles, yellow pine floors, and large windows.

More than just a home, the house became the center of the family business. A tiled storeroom in the basement was filled with stacks of furs, guns, wampum, and bolts of cloth. Margaret ran a sawmill and sold valuable lumber. Eventually she and Frederick amassed about 57,000 acres, buying land from neighbors and Native Americans, including most of present-day Westchester County. The location allowed them to avoid English scrutiny, as well as taxes, for smaller vessels could secretly dock below the house to load and unload goods.

Even farther from English rule, the family spent April through June each year at their home in Albany, the center of the fur trade. A bill of lading for one of their ships offers a glimpse of their fur inventory for sale to European markets: 1,713 beaver pelts, the most valuable of all the furs; 502 bear pelts; 1,550 buckskins; 46 cowhides; 1,250 standard foxes and 53 gray foxes; 94 timber minks; 1,200 cats (bobcats); 1,100 otter; and others. The same ship returned to New York carrying linen, swords, musket barrels, tools, books, and wool.

Little is known of what Margaret thought or felt, but she must have been a woman of strong opinions, strong character, and bountiful energy. Court records show that in 1675 Frederick had two clergymen from the Dutch Reformed Church come to the house. He'd had a falling out with his wife and hoped the churchmen might persuade Margaret to reconcile with him. Margaret greeted the men with sharp words, shouting: "You have the devil in you!"

Margaret often took one of her children with her on the long sea voyages to Amsterdam, and not surprisingly her sons entered the family business as young men. Passengers on one of her ships described her as "miserable covetous," displaying "terrible parsimony," and calling Margaret arrogant and abrasive. Perhaps the two men who scribbled down their thoughts on Margaret disliked the fact that a woman was in charge of all the cargo on board. And, as ship owner, Margaret outranked even the captain. Margaret had spent her whole life in commercial affairs, making every penny count, and when she sent sailors out in a rowboat on the ocean to retrieve a mop that had fallen overboard, she probably did seem to suffer from "terrible parsimony." A male servant on board, named Jan, seemed overly familiar and intimate with Margaret, and speculation ran rampant that the two were involved in an illicit affair.

Margaret and Frederick added to their empire in 1674 when they jumped on a new hot trade commodity—sugar, the sweet addiction of North Americans and Europeans. The couple purchased a sugar plantation, Spring Head, in Barbados. The Philipses carried European wines, tobacco, lumber, grain, and salted beef to the island. They filled their empty ships with cone-shaped blocks of sugar and molasses (a sugar by-product) for making rum, as well as tropical fruits, parrots, and conch meant for New York and Europe.

Sugar production depended on the sweat of enslaved African laborers. The first slaves had been carried to Barbados in 1627, one year after the first African slaves had arrived in Manhattan. Not surprisingly, Margaret and Frederick entered the trade in this human commodity in 1684, when Margaret's ship, *Charles*, left England with a load of shackles included in the cargo hold. The captain sailed to Angola and there picked up 146 African prisoners of war. Some of the captives died on the 3,500-mile ocean crossing to Barbados. But the captain sold 105 of the survivors. The remaining nine Africans sailed to New York to work on Philipse-owned lands. In one stroke Margaret became a slave trader and a slave owner; both made perfect economic sense to her.

Like most colonial women, Margaret Hardenbroeck lived as wife, mother, and keeper of the house. But those realms revolved around, even paled against, Margaret's true calling as a colonial she-merchant. Remarkable for a woman of her time, Margaret built her own fortune and sailed her own ships to trade in the great cities of London and Amsterdam. She died in 1691, at age 54. Her rise in Manhattan was probably undreamt of when she'd first gone ashore all those years before, eager to serve as her cousin's factor. Back then, she'd tried and failed to collect a debt owed him, but vowed she would soon try again. "I did my best," she wrote him, summing up the motto of her life in those four simple words.

The Journey of
Sarah Kemble Knight

"Monday, Octb'r. ye second, 1704.—About three o'clock afternoon, I begun my Journey from Boston to New-Haven; being about two Hundred Mile."

SARAH KEMBLE KNIGHT's ultimate destination was New York City, where she had business settling a relative's estate. In her journal she recorded the five-month round-trip adventure: hours on horseback, traversing rough roads and dangerous rivers, sleeping in seedy inns and welcoming homes. At age 38 Sarah was not a young woman, middle-aged by any standard in 1704. She undertook such a harrowing journey because duty called, and Sarah Kemble Knight had proven her worth as a businesswoman.

Born in Boston in 1666 and raised in a merchant family, Sarah married Richard Knight sometime around 1689. The couple had one child, a daughter named Elizabeth. Referred to as Madame Knight—a sign of respect—Sarah probably shared the duties of her husband's business ventures before his death in 1703.

As a widow, Sarah proved herself a capable businesswoman. Over the years she ran a writing school, owned a stationery shop, managed a boardinghouse, learned enough law to handle legal matters including settling estates, and owned several farms. Then, in October 1704, she made the journey to New York. Her travel journal captured Sarah Knight's view of the world, often laced with her sense of humor, and it is through this record she still lives on the pages of history, vibrant as the year she penned her thoughts.

Sarah traveled with post carriers, meeting them at a mail stop to join their journey, or she hired guides at taverns and inns along the way. She paid the men for their time and trouble in coin as well as a drink at the end of the night. They traveled fast, the post riders often stopping to wait for Sarah "with my weary bones" to catch up. At night, the horses slowed to a jog or walk, picking their way through the pitch blackness of the forest with only stars and the moon to light their path. The ghostly glimmerings "rendered every Object formidable," noted Sarah. "Each lifeless Trunk, with its shatter'd Limbs, appear'd an Armed Enymie' and every little stump like a Ravenous devourer." One night as they reached the top of a hill, the moon broke through the clouds, inspiring Sarah to write a poem:

Fair Cynthia [the moon], all the Homage that I may
Unto a Creature, unto thee I pay;
In Lonesome woods to meet so kind a guide,
To Mee's more worth than all the world beside.

Day after day, for five months, Sarah faced hard riding and dangers that required all her courage and endurance, both mentally and physically. It was quite a feat for anyone, man or woman, but certainly a daring adventure for a lady. Sarah endured many perils on the road—a swamp wreathed in fog, a swollen river, steep hills to climb and descend.

At one river, the post rider hired a boy to row Sarah across in a small canoe. Water lapped at the top of the shallow boat, threatening to capsize it, while Sarah clung to the sides, not daring to move, white-knuckled and terrified. The post carrier rode through the water, leading Sarah's horse. Imagined images of her "Approaching fate" frightened Sarah at river crossings. "Sometimes seeing my self drowning," she wrote, "otherwhiles drowned, and at the best like a holy Sister just come out of a Spiritual Bath in dripping Garments."

Another time, afraid and exhausted, she said good-bye to the post riders at a rushing river, too fearful to cross. Instead she asked for shelter at a nearby cottage—"one of the wretchedest I ever saw a habitation for human creatures"—and waited for the water to fall. Once, her horse slipped and nearly tumbled into the water foaming under a bridge. Even without water hazards, most roads greeted riders with rocks, stumps, and mountain passages, "very disagreeable to my tired carcass," noted Sarah.

Each night Sarah arrived at an inn or house, exhausted from her day's adventures and ready for supper and bed. While Sarah was often "very civilly Received, and courteously entertained, in a clean comfortable House," other nights her lodgings proved less desirable, her standards of cleanliness, comfort, and cooking shockingly not met. While staying at a French family's home she noted the meal cooked "so contrary to my notion of Cookery, that I hastned to Bed superless." Another woman served her pickled mutton; the vinegary aroma was so strong that neither Sarah nor her guide could eat it. "We left it, and pd sixpence a piece for our Dinners, wch was only smell."

While most people opened their homes to travelers, Sarah and her guide were turned away one night during a howling snowstorm by "a surly old shoe Creature, not worthy the name of woman, though the weather was so stormy none but shee would have turnd out a Dogg." Luckily, the woman's grown son took Sarah in, letting her sleep in a loft on a bed warmed by a hot stone at her feet. Cold, sick, and vomiting, she endured until morning.

Innkeepers tried to offer Sarah, a rare female traveler, her own space—usually a small lean-to built onto the inn—where the bedstead took up most of the room and household junk spilled from the corners. Sarah fell into bed, so tired but often unable to sleep on the hard mattresses covered in threadbare blankets. "My poor bones complained bitterly not being use to such Lodgings," she noted on one occasion. Many nights, tavern merrymakers and loud talkers just beyond her wall kept her awake.

One night a heated political squabble permeated the thin walls of her chamber. Roaring voices and thundering blows upon the table "pierced my very head. I heartily frettd, and wish't 'um tongue tyed." Sarah sat up, lit the bedside candle, and "fell to my old way of composing my Resentments," she wrote, furiously penning a poem.

> I ask thy Aid, O Potent Rum!
> To Charm these wrangling Topers Dum.
> Thou has their Giddy Brains possest . . .
> And I, poor I, can get no rest.
> Intoxicate them with thy fumes:
> O still their Tongues till morning comes!

"And I know not but my wishes took effect," she reported, "for the dispute soon ended" with another drink, "and so Good night!"

Another night, a female innkeeper, "a pretty full mouth'd old creature," entertained Sarah's fellow traveler, a doctor, with a long list of "complaints of her bodily infirmities; and whispered to him so lou'd, that all ye House had as full a hearing as he."

At one inn, the innkeeper's daughter couldn't get over the fact that Sarah had undertaken her journey. "I never see a woman on the Rode [road] so Dreadfull late. . . . Who are You?

Where are You going?" and when it turned out the girl knew Sarah's guide, she lit into him, demanding to know what he was doing with Sarah. Finally Sarah had enough of the foolish girl, who had not even asked her to sit down. "I told her shee treated me very Rudely, and I did not think it my duty to answer her unmannerly Questions."

As she rode through Massachusetts, Connecticut, and New York, Sarah filled her journal with observations about the people she met. She commented that the Puritans of New Haven had been too rigid in their laws, even whipping people for "a harmless Kiss or Innocent merriment among the Young people." She found others in Connecticut "too indulgent (especially ye farmers) to their slaves . . . permitting ym to sit at Table and eat with them . . . and into the dish goes the black hoof as freely as the white hand." Men, she noted, chewed and spit tobacco "as long as they'r eyes are open."

She found New York City a pleasant place with stately brick buildings, and she admired the Dutch fashion for tiles around the fireplace and hearth. New Yorkers did not keep the Sabbath as strictly as Bostonians, Sarah noted. The English dressed very fashionably, but she found the Dutch women "go loose" wearing less constrictive clothing, and wore many rings and earrings. People drank quite "Liberally" and enjoyed riding sleighs in the winter: "they fly with great swiftness and some are so furious that they'le turn out of the path for none except a Loaden Cart."

In December Sarah began her journey from New York back to Boston. In Fairfield, Connecticut, Sarah found a hot dispute between the wealthy citizens and their minister. A sheep industry thrived in the town, "whose very Dung brings them great gain." Money from manure sales paid the minister's salary, and the townspeople begrudged that, wrote Sarah, "preferring their Dung before their minister."

In early March Sarah reached Massachusetts. She tried to push hard to get home, but her horse collapsed from exhaustion and Sarah lost time while she found another. The rivers ran high, and horses and riders labored over muddy roads. On March 3 Sarah arrived home, "where I found my aged and tender mother and my Dear and only Child in good health with open arms redy to receive me." Having heard no word of Sarah's fate for five months, friends and relatives flocked to the house, anxious to hear Sarah's travel adventures.

In 1713 Sarah moved with her daughter, Elizabeth, and son-in-law to Connecticut. She continued her business ventures, living in Norwich or on one of several farms she owned in New London. Her stature earned her a designated pew in the Norwich church meetinghouse. A Norwich town record from 1718 recorded that Sarah was "taxed twenty shillings for selling strong drink to the Indians," but the record noted that Sarah denied the charge and "accuses her maid, Ann Clark, of the fact."

Sarah died in September 1727, leaving a large estate of about £1,800 to Elizabeth. Her tombstone, elaborately carved, speaks

Tombstone, Here Lyeth The Body of Mrs. Sarah Knight.
Courtesy of Cricket Luke and Vivien Hunnicutt

to her well-placed status and still stands in Connecticut's oldest cemetery. Sarah Knight's journal, meant only for herself, family, and friends, was rediscovered and published in 1825. Within the pages, she provided a lasting record of one woman's harrowing journey and witty observations through the wilds of colonial New England.

6

꧁꧂

Daughters of Eve

Read often the Matrimonial Service, and overlook not the important word OBEY.

—*advice to wives from the* **Virginia Gazette,** *1737*

IN 1687 SARAH HARRISON and Doctor James Blair stood in front of a minister reciting their marriage vows. But when the minister reached the point in the ceremony where the wife promises to obey her husband, Sarah quietly answered, "No obey." In disbelief, the minister repeated the vow. Three times Sarah refused, replying only: "No obey." Finally the exasperated clergyman turned to Sarah's groom. Doctor Blair nodded his permission and the wedding continued. But the bride's glaring omission filled the air.

In the 1600s and 1700s, a response like Sarah Harrison's flabbergasted most people and set tongues wagging. From childhood on, girls learned they'd one day obey a husband, just as they obeyed a father during childhood. No young woman grew up thinking she might remain single—marriage and child-birth were a woman's very purpose on Earth. Everything she absorbed prepared her to be a wife and mother.

"ONE PERSON IN THE LAW"

A single woman could own and sell property and leave property to her heirs. A single woman could sue and be sued in court. She could make contracts, earn wages, and run a business.

But all that changed the minute she married, for marriage swallowed a wife whole into her husband's identity. Under English law, which also governed the colonies, "the very being or legal existence of the woman is suspended during the marriage." Her life was "consolidated into that of the husband; under whose wing, protection, and cover, she performs everything." All that a wife possessed, right down to her shift, belonged to her husband.

Marriage involved duties for each partner. The husband provided a home, financial support, and protection. Society expected he'd treat his wife with respect and not rule as a tyrant. In return, the wife ran his home efficiently, raised his children, comforted him, and assisted him in all things. Although a wife might provide input and advice, her husband made all decisions. A good wife submitted to his choices, not because he forced her but because in doing so she chose to follow God's path.

Legal standings aside, most colonists' views on men, women, and marriage derived from the Bible, which recorded that the first man, Adam, "ruled over" his wife, Eve. In 1643 Thomas Dudley advised his daughter Mercy that God "gracyously placed thy good husband here" for her to "submytt [submit] and trust." Wrote John Winthrop:

> The woman's own choice makes such a man her husband, yet being so chosen, he is her lord and She is to be

subject to him, yet in a way of liberty, not of bondage, and a true wife accounts her subjection her honor and freedom.

Many couples, like John and Margaret Winthrop, believed that spiritual and physical oneness created an ideal marriage. Husbands and wives should have "a special Care and Tenderness one of another," explained author Samuel Willard (1640–1707). Anne Bradstreet celebrated the love in her marriage through poetry. But even love for a husband might be carried too far. Mehitable Parkman wrote her husband in June of 1683: "Mrs. Mechison tells me often she fears that I love you more than god."

FEMALES AND SIN

Marriage served as the rock of a stable society. It created order and restrained sexual missteps. Everyone had a duty to marry. Maryland even taxed bachelors, since a man without a wife and children shirked his public duty. An unmarried woman not only failed to meet society's expectations but also added to her family's burdens—her father or adult brothers had to continue feeding, clothing, and bearing responsibility for the wretched girl.

Marriage was thought to shelter both men and women against wickedness. People believed that once Eve seduced Adam into sin in the Garden of Eden, she branded all women as troublemakers and temptresses. Books and sermons depicted these colonial "Daughters of Eve" as "the weaker vessel," easily misled, tempted by flattery, and given to "extravagance." People acknowledged that men contributed to sin, too. But it was believed a male often sinned only when enticed by females—or under the influence of alcohol.

According to a popular advice book George Saville, the Earl of Halifax, wrote for his daughter, men had "the larger share of *Reason* bestow'd upon them." And a male needed every ounce of his intellect to guide a woman's actions. "Your *Sex* wanteth our *Reason* for your *Conduct*," explained Halifax. Women also required men's "*Strength* for your *Protection*." In return, men "wanteth" women's "*Gentleness* to soften, and to entertain us."

Colonial citizens believed men could misbehave "with out contaminating the mind." But women had to be "virtuous" or else become "utterly undone." A double standard existed even for unfaithful spouses. "A woman who breaks her marriage vows," claimed one male writer, "is much more criminal than a man who does it." After all, a husband wanted to be sure that a son born to his wife actually was his own flesh and blood. It wouldn't do to have another man's child inherit the family property.

COURTSHIP AND WEDDINGS

With marriage of utmost importance, young people courted at dances, barbecues, and get-togethers such as cornhuskings and barn raisings. They met at church and at parties hosted by relatives. A young woman might flirt, but she'd better also wear an air of modesty sweet as any perfume.

While daughters in poorer families had some freedom to follow their hearts, wealthier parents actively screened suitors, scrutinizing bank accounts, property, and family connections. Marriage was a financial bargain, their child an asset. Courtship often did not begin until the two fathers exchanged letters detailing financial information.

A girl's father stated up front what money or property his daughter would receive as her marriage portion. Daniel Parke agreed to let his daughter Frances marry the son of John Custis in 1705, "if my daughter likes him." Parke wrote Custis that he'd base his daughter's wedding portion on the young man's own fortune: "I will give her upon her marriage with him, half as much as he can make it appear he is worth." Colonial

Rural Courtship, engraving published in London around 1761.
The Colonial Williamsburg Foundation, Museum Purchase

newspapers often broadcast the juicy details of a wedding portion. In 1749, the *South Carolina Gazette* reported that Susannah
Seabrook was "endowed with all agreeable Accomplishments
and a Fortune of £15,000."

What made a girl the perfect wife for an upper-class marriage? In August 1732 Massachusetts governor Jonathan Belcher wrote his son a list of qualifications. The young woman must have "Strict Vertue" and a "Good Nature." She should be "Agreeable (no matter whether beautiful)" with "passable good sense (no matter whether over-quick & sharp)." But most dear to this colonial father's heart, a future daughter-in-law must provide "a Plentifull fortune."

With property at stake, most colonial parents believed young women were easily swayed by roguish flattery and therefore poor judges of a man's character. Most often a daughter obeyed her parents' wishes when she selected a husband. Colonial fathers were not above disinheriting or shunning children for marrying against their wishes.

The father of 16-year-old Evelyn Byrd, William Byrd II, forbade her from seeing the man she loved. In a furious letter William commanded Evelyn "never more to meet, speak or write to that gentleman, or give him an opportunity to see, speak or write to you." If Evelyn married the young man, she'd get no money from her parent. And if Evelyn's love turned sour, her

Portrait of Evelyn Byrd, artist unidentified, painted in London around 1725.
The Colonial Williamsburg Foundation, Museum Purchase

father would offer no comfort. "To whom will you fly in your distress," he asked, "when all the world will upbraid you with having acted an idiot?"

Evelyn dutifully obeyed and broke off the courtship. By her 20th birthday, her father jokingly referred to her as "one of the most antick [antique] Virgins." Evelyn Byrd died unwed "in the 29th year of her age." William Byrd acknowledged Evelyn's attributes on the white marble slab of her tomb:

The various & excellent Endowments
of Nature Improved and perfected
by an accomplished Education:
Formed her,
For the Happyness of her friends;
For an Ornament of her Country.
Alas reader!
We can detain nothing however Valued
From unrelenting Death:
Beauty, Fortune or Exalted Honor!
See here a Proof!
And be reminded by this awful Tomb
That every worldly Comfort fleets away.

Unlike Evelyn, Judy Carter defied her father and wed "against her duty." Her father, Robert, the wealthiest man in Virginia, banished Judy from his sight for two years after the elopement. But Judy's marriage proved unhappy, and her father relented, offering the "poor offending" girl a bit of money "for personal necessaries." But he made sure to "give nothing" that her husband might claim.

If a girl opposed her parents' choice, she had a duty to speak up. Otherwise she risked being an unhappy and disloyal wife in the future. "They that marry where they affect [love] not," went a Puritan saying, "will affect [love] where they marry not."

A young woman greeted a marriage proposal with dignity, words of gratitude, and a firm reminder that she must consult her parents. One magazine writer offered advice in 1711 about how to keep from appearing unladylike. "A virtuous woman should reject the first offer of marriage," observed the author, even if the girl's heart was crying "Yes!" But, the young lady shouldn't say no to the same man too often. "I would advise [not] to persist in refusing what they secretly approve."

Most weddings were simple affairs in the bride's home or maybe at her church. A frolic of food, drink, and dancing followed the ceremony and might go on for days, especially in the South. In Puritan New England marriage was a civil contract, officiated by a judge or a magistrate instead of a clergyman. Dancing and frolicking, of course, played no part in a Puritan wedding.

YOUNGER BRIDES, LARGER FAMILIES

In the early days of the colonies, many women had indentures to serve before they could wed. By the time their indenture ended, many of these women had reached their 25th birthdays, and some were even older. This was considered old for a first marriage, especially with the odds high that a woman would die by her 35th birthday. In the disease-infested Chesapeake colonies, many women bore fewer than four children before they died—a small number for the time.

Enslaved African women also bore few children in the early years of the colonial era, sometimes as few as one or two. Many black women in slavery suffered from exhaustion and malnutrition, which affected their ability to bear children. Some lived on farms with few other Africans, limiting their choice of partners, though some pregnancies resulted from sexual abuse at the hands of a woman's master. Other women rebelled and refused to bear children in an alien, harsh world.

By the 1700s, however, times were changing for both black and white women. Many women of marriage age had been born in the colonies. Life expectancy for women stretched as they escaped the harsh years of hardening to a new climate and rough work. Fewer white women had indentures to serve and began marrying at a younger age. It was not uncommon for 18th-century girls to wed by their 16th birthdays.

Earlier marriages meant an unmarried girl was "reckoned a stale maid" by age 25. The jabs at unmarried women continued

A woman depicted as an old maid, or spinster, in a British cartoon, 1777.
Library of Congress, LC-USZ62-97560

throughout the 18th century. Newspapers depicted "old maids" as harridans jealous of every married woman. One newspaper stingingly summed up the situation. "An old maid is one of the most cranky, ill-natured, maggotty, peevish . . . good for nothing creatures," it said. "[She] enters the world to take up room, not to make room for others."

CHILDBIRTH

Since a woman's main duty was to bear children, people thought the best mothers were those with the most offspring. Blame for fertility issues rested with a woman, who must have wondered why God had forsaken her. Anne Bradstreet faced what she thought of as a barren and childless darkness during the first years of her marriage, before giving birth to a son.

Most women spent their adult lives in a never-ending cycle of pregnancy, labor, and nursing. It was common for women to have 10 to 20 pregnancies. Many women were still having babies even after their grown daughters began bearing children.

People explained women's labor pains as God's punishment of Eve, quoting from the Bible: "In sorrow thou shalt bring forth children." Women shouldn't complain of their suffering, however. Noted one minister, she should accept that "the Sin of my Mother [Eve], which is also my Sin, has brought all this upon me."

Going into labor meant being "brought to bed," "lying in," or arriving at "the moment of travail." Women of every status relied on other women for comfort and help. A midwife, experienced in matters of birth, attended the mother. Some midwives delivered hundreds of babies during their careers. Female relatives, friends, and neighbors also attended the birth, munching "groaning cakes" and sipping "groaning beer," special items meant to nourish mother and guests through the ordeal. Husbands played no part other than running errands and waiting.

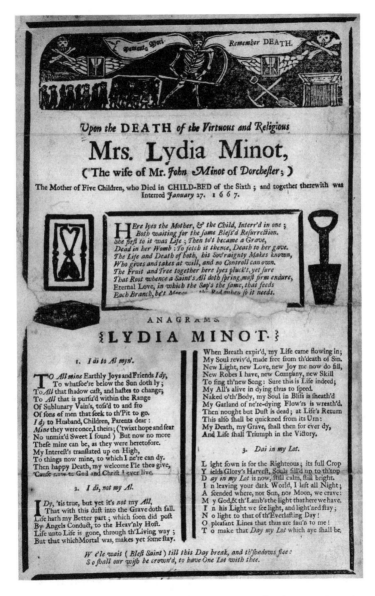

A broadside: *Upon the Death of the Virtuous and Religious Mrs. Lydia Minot.* Cambridge, Massachusetts: Printed by Samuel Green, 1668. *Courtesy of the Massachusetts Historical Society*

Childbirth proved a dangerous task, and many women died from delivery complications such as bleeding and infections. Some women were just worn out, weakened from their numerous pregnancies. Anticipating the approaching birth of one of her children, a melancholy Anne Bradstreet wrote her husband wondering, "How soon, my Dear, death may my steps attend."

Tombstone inscriptions and newspaper notices recounted many sad tales: "Died in Child Birth in the 33d Year of her age, Mrs. Sarah Carlyle." "Of a Miscarriage of Twins, died here in the 24th Year of her age . . . Mrs. Calhoun." "Underneath lies what was mortal of Mrs. Margaret Edwards. . . . She Died in Travail [labor] with her tenth Child Aged 34 years."

Babies, swaddled like little mummies, fit into a busy colonial household as best they could. Wealthy women had servants to help with child care and housework. But most women returned to household duties shortly after delivery. Eventually, as a family welcomed new members, older children helped their mothers with young ones.

Society viewed mothers as the more affectionate, nurturing, and fondly indulgent parent. To balance this perceived feminine weakness, children required a father's guidance, authority, and discipline. In reality, however, most mothers were so busy with constant chores they had little time to either spoil or discipline individual children. Only the wealthiest women, such as Eliza Pinckney of South Carolina, could study books on child rearing and create plans for the education of their children.

"NOW WIVES"

Dangers in childbirth, rampant disease, deadly accidents, and exhausting work meant death might snatch a mother, father, or child at any time. But society depended upon marriage and the duties shared by wife and husband. Not surprisingly, most people remarried at least once after the loss of their first spouse.

Four or five marriages were not uncommon. And remarriage often occurred quite quickly. In one breath, people offered sympathy for the loss of a spouse and in the next breath offered congratulations on a new marriage.

A man might lose a wife and remarry so often that his children referred to his "now wife." Mothers facing childbirth or a deadly illness worried that a future stepmother might neglect the children she left behind. Writing of her own possible death, Anne Bradstreet begged her husband to "Look to my little Babes. . . . These O protect from step-dame's injury."

With resources often scarce, some stepmothers had little interest in their new husbands' previous offspring. In some cases they treated stepchildren as mere servants or banished them elsewhere to work. Who inherited land, money, and goods from the father was often disputed by the children of his several marriages. The wicked stepmother of fairy tales was not just a character in literature—Charles Perrault's version of *Cinderella* was published in France 1697—but a reality for some families.

"NAUGHTY FURIOUS HOUSEWIVES"

Realistically, wives did not always obey and husbands did not always treat their spouses with respect. Colonial mates argued, criticized, and ignored each other. The marriage of John Custis and Frances Parke in 1706, so carefully planned by their fathers, dissolved into such hostility that by 1714 the couple drew up a legal document defining expected behaviors. Frances agreed to return John's money, plate—all his dishes, utensils, silver, pewter, or gold—and anything else she'd taken and use "no vile names or use bad language" to him. John agreed to not abuse Frances and to give her half his estate's profits to run the household. They agreed to be "lovingly together and behave themselves as a good husband and wife ought to do." Frances died that same year and John, unlike most men, refused to marry again.

In 1744 Susannah Cooper petitioned the Virginia House of Burgesses for help, claiming she had not heard from her runaway husband in 20 years. Furthermore, he'd recklessly spent the money *she'd* brought to their marriage. Susannah asked the house members to grant her the right to sell property and make contracts, even though legally she remained a married woman without the power to do these things. The members agreed to her petition.

Susannah Cooper had not sought a divorce, which was rarely an option for ending an unhappy marriage. Between 1664 and 1775, no divorce was granted in New York. In South Carolina only the governor and his council could dissolve a marriage. In New England, divorce was slightly easier since marriage was viewed as a civil contract. Most often, courts ordered sparring spouses to reform and behave, even in cases where husbands physically abused their wives.

No one questioned that children belonged to the father. Elizabeth Byrd was heartsick when her husband sent their baby to live with his meddling mother. "Poor dear babe," wrote Elizabeth. "But Sir, your Orders must be obeyed whatever reluctance I find thereby."

Newspapers carried frequent notices about wives who "eloped from" their husbands. The men rushed to publicly announce they would no longer pay an eloped wife's debts. They charged their wives with behaving "in a very imprudent manner," or that she was "highly undutiful and disaffectionate." Worse was the woman who'd transformed into a "naughty furious Housewife." Some abandoned husbands accused a wife of stealing her own dresses and petticoats when she left. And of course, most husbands insisted they had no clue why their wives had fled.

Sometimes a wife returned the favor. "John Cantwell has the impudence to advertise me in the Papers," wrote wife Sarah of South Carolina, "cautioning all Persons against crediting me;

he never had any Credit till he married me. . . : I never eloped, I
went away before his Face when he beat me."

PROVIDING FOR A WIFE

Legally, when a husband died, his wife was entitled to one-third
of his estate. In addition, a husband usually left his wife her jewelry in his will. Peyton Randolph, a Virginia lawyer and politi-
cian left his wife, Betty, not only her rings and other jewelry; he
also left the lady her clothes, which were a pricey commodity
and technically belonged to his estate.

Typically, a husband granted his widow the use of their home
and belongings until her own death. But many widows lost control of their former homes when an oldest son took over. If the
couple had young children on the husband's death, guardianship
might be granted to the mother. Just as often, though, a friend
of the father or a male relative served as the guardian and was
responsible for the child's finances and the education of any sons.

If a widow remarried, her new husband took over the former husband's estate and controlled her "thirds." George Washington became a wealthy man when he married the recently
widowed Martha Custis. Many husbands made provisions for a
wife's remarriage. "My wife Alice to Have and enjoy the Land I
live on for her widowhood," wrote Mathias Marriott of Virginia
in his will. "After her death or remarriage the Land is to return
to my son."

Some husbands rewarded their wives for a lifetime of loyalty.
Benjamin Harrison left his wife more than her thirds. "She hath
at all times behaved in a most dutiful and affectionate manner
to me and all ways been assisting through my whole affairs,"
Harrison explained. Samuel Cobb, a poor Virginia farmer, could
not provide for both his wife and his grown children. He chose
his wife. "I do think it my Duty to provide for a Wife now in
Decline of life who so well Deserved it from me," he said.

PUNISHMENTS

Even goodwives remained daughters of Eve. Colonial people believed in physical corrections for wrongdoers, and that included women. Females faced a wide range of punishments for various crimes, including fines, branding, whipping, burning, and hanging.

People considered the crime of gossiping a female sin. "Brabling women," read a 1662 Virginia law, "often . . . scandalize their neighbors for which their poore husbands are often brought into chargeable and vexatious suites." Officials marched a gossip to the nearest pond, tied her to a stool on the end of a long wooden arm, and ducked her underwater five or six times.

Other common charges against women included bearing a child out of wedlock and having an affair. In these cases, the woman usually suffered a stronger punishment than the man involved. If she couldn't pay the fine, she instead endured a public whipping.

Some women faced death sentences and tried, like condemned pirate Anne Bonny, to stall their executions by "pleading their bellies" in a claim of pregnancy. A group of matrons examined the woman to see if she really was with child. If so, officials postponed the execution until after the birth.

WITCHCRAFT IN SALEM VILLAGE

Witchcraft was a crime charged almost exclusively against women. For most of the 17th century, authorities only occasionally prosecuted women thought to be witches. But in January 1692, witch hunts began in earnest in Salem Village, Massachusetts.

Massachusetts faced stressful and changing times. Divisions within the colony led the English king to revoke Massachusetts Bay's charter and appoint a royal governor to rule instead.

Waves of newcomers lacked the Puritan zeal and faith of the first generations of colonists who'd built New England, causing more strife.

Decades of brutal frontier wars with Native Americans had shaken people's faith. Refugees from frontier towns described horrors of mutilation by the "black Indians," words synonymous for many with Satan. New Englanders had long associated the wilderness and native people with evil, and they believed firmly that an invisible evil surrounded their own good society. The world of 1692, with recent Native American attacks to the north, appeared in upheaval, the devil's hand unleashed.

In mid-January 1692, Abigail Williams, age 11, and her cousin Betty Parris, age 9, showed signs of a strange illness and erratic behavior. The girls exhibited bite marks and pinch marks that seemed beyond anything seen from a seizure or fit. Doctor William Griggs determined an "Evil Hand" tormented the children. Under questioning Abigail and Betty named who tormented them: on February 29 complaints were registered against Tituba, a West Indian slave in the Reverend Samuel Parris's household, and, on Tituba's word, Sarah Osborne and Sarah Good.

The fear of witchcraft sent ripples of horror through Salem Village and the surrounding villages of Essex County. Tituba confessed to signing the devil's book, flying on a pole, and pinching and choking some of the afflicted girls. She also later claimed the Reverend Parris beat her and she'd been told to confess to witchcraft. But her confession, and the fact that she named Osborne and Good as other witches, added to the hysteria sweeping Salem Village. Her words seemed clear evidence that witches had infested the countryside; these devil's helpmates must be purged.

The "afflicted girls" claimed apparitions of witches visited them. These specters tortured the girls into fits by pinching them, biting them, choking them, and other forms of torments.

A woman faces the court, accused of practicing witchcraft.
U.S. History Images

The girls claimed they saw the witches consorting with the devil, drinking blood, reading the devil's book. Accusations flew fast and furious. The girls, supported by adults and clergy, accused a handful of women and men of witchcraft. In a world where normally young girls and teenaged female servants would be given scarcely a thought, the afflicted young women became the center of attention, their every move watched and recorded by the men of their households, ministers, and magistrates.

The same girls accused many, with more voices joining the chorus and adding to the accusations. Abigail Williams made 41 complaints. Twelve-year-old Ann Putnam made 53 complaints and gave formal testimony 28 times. Mary Walcott, age 17, made 69 complaints and testified 28 times.

Witch hysteria swept through Salem Village and Essex County. Older and poorer women, many widowed and without protection, proved easy marks for the finger-pointing. The influence of adults must have played a strong role in who the impressionable girls accused. Through the summer and fall of 1692, Salem Village officials examined, indicted, tried, and executed 19 people—14 of them women—as witches. The jails filled with more than 100 others awaiting trial, and several people died in jail.

Once in court, judges assumed the guilt of the accused and fired questions based on the depositions of the afflicted. The people accused of witchcraft helplessly defended themselves, struggling to answer questions that had no answers. How many times could you deny you were a witch? Some confessed, naming others as part of the devil's brigade in Essex County. The examinations often disintegrated into a circus as the afflicted girls howled with pain, lay twitching on the floor, and demanded what Satan—seen as a black man—whispered in the accused persons' ear. Many of the accused, like Martha Corey, could only repeat, "I am an innocent person. I never had to do with witchcraft."

As the frightening number of arrests soared, opposition to the executions grew. How did anyone know this whole thing wasn't itself a plot by Satan? In October Governor William Phips distanced himself from the proceedings. He ordered no further arrests and soon ended the special court meant to try witches. Seeking answers, he stressed his growing belief that Satan could raise apparitions in the form of innocent persons and use those to inflict injury. By spring 1693 the trials had ended and the jails cleared.

On January 14, 1696, a day of fasting and prayer, juror Samuel Sewall publicly apologized for his role, acknowledging God's anger against Massachusetts for the witchcraft trials. Others too asked pardon for their shame. Twelve former jurors blamed the horror on the devil: "We ourselves were not capable to understand, nor able to withstand the mysterious delusions of the Powers of Darkness."

In 1706 Ann Putnam, now in her 20s, stood with her head bowed before the church congregation and read a confession, probably written by the new village minister. Ann begged forgiveness, claimed she'd been deluded by the devil, and wished she could die for her part in the accusations and trials. She was given communion, having made her penance, and died unmarried in 1715. She was the only accuser to make any public statement about her role. Sadly, too many had died, unable to defend themselves against the girls and the adults who'd supported the accusers, as they screamed, pointed, and charged their neighbors of consorting with the devil.

Martha Corey
Accused of Witchcraft

THREE WOMEN HAD ALREADY been accused of practicing witchcraft in Salem Village, Massachusetts, when a constable
appeared on the doorstep of Giles Corey, a farmer. The constable carried a signed warrant, dated March 19, 1692, for the arrest
of Giles's wife, Martha, charging she had "Comitted sundry acts
of Witchcraft."

Martha's arrest shook a community already fearful that the
devil and his witch minions stalked the town. The first women
accused by young Abigail Williams and Betty Parris had lived
on the margins of society, considered unsavory persons and
outcasts—one a slave, the others poor. But Goodwife Martha
Corey lived on a prosperous farm. People knew her as a woman
of faith, elected to church membership in 1690.

Martha's past held one glaring blemish. Before her first marriage to Henry Rich, she'd given birth to an illegitimate son.
The young man now lived with Martha and Giles, her second husband, a constant reminder to others of Martha's past

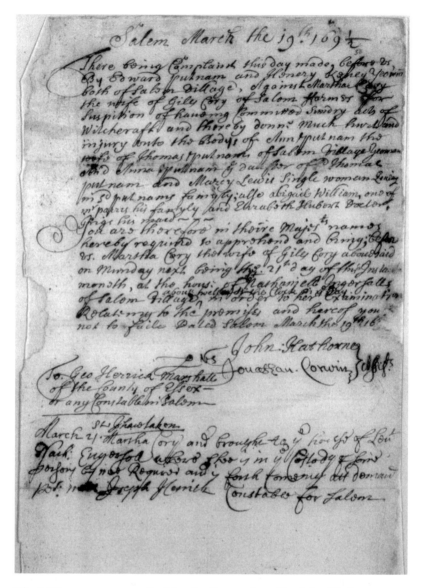

The 1692 arrest warrant for Martha Corey, signed by John Hathorne.
*From the records of the Court of Oyer and Terminer, 1692, property of the Supreme
Judicial Court, Division of Archives and Records Preservation on deposit at the Peabody
Essex Museum, Salem, Massachusetts*

indiscretion. This may have led some to question not only Martha's goodness but her recent election to the church, too.

The accusations leading to Martha's arrest began gathering in early March like thunderclouds soon to unleash the storm. Twelve-year-old Ann Putnam had told her parents and her uncle, Edward Putnam, that "goode Corie did often appear to her and tortor her by pinching and other wayes." Along with the court clerk, Ezekiel Cheever, Edward Putnam prepared to visit Martha on Saturday, March 12. But the men stopped first at Thomas Putnam's home to see Ann. They asked the girl what clothes Martha's specter had worn, to make sure Ann "was not mistaken in the person." Ann told the men she did not know what Goody Corey wore for Martha had blinded her, but "told her that her name was Corie and that shee should see her no more . . . because she should not tell us what cloathes shee had on."

Edward Putnam later recalled that as soon as they entered her house Martha cried: "You are come to talke with me about being a witch but I am none I cannot helpe peoples talking of me." They had come, answered Edward, because an "afflicted person" had complained about Martha. Martha then eagerly asked if Ann told them what clothes she had on. The men replied no—Ann had told them Martha blinded her. Martha "made but little answer to this," claimed Edward Putnam, "but seemed to smile at it as if shee had showed us a pretty trick."

They discussed how God and the church were "dishonored by this means," but Martha seemed more concerned, recalled Edward, with stopping the spread of gossip, that people should "not say thus of her." How could they think her guilty of witchcraft, Martha demanded, when "she had made a profession of Christ and rejoyeced to go and hear the word of god and the like"? Edward answered that an outward profession of good did not clear her from being a witch "for it had often been so in the wourld that witches had crept into the churches."

On Monday the Putnams asked Martha to come to their home. Edward Putnam later testified about the visit. No sooner did Martha arrive than Ann charged Martha that she had hurt her by witchcraft. The girl then fell into a fit, choking, her feet and hands twisted, her body writhing in agony. Martha bewitched her, Ann cried, and immediately Ann's tongue was drawn from her mouth and her teeth clamped down upon it so she could not speak.

When at last the girl could talk again she pointed at Martha, crying that a yellow bird sucked the flesh between Goody Corey's forefinger and middle finger. Edward Putnam said Martha rubbed the spot and Ann was once more blinded and could see nothing. Everyone in the Putnam household knew this yellow bird must be Martha's familiar, the supernatural creature, a demon, that assisted Goody Corey in her devilry.

Ann turned to the large open fireplace and claimed she saw a man roasting on a spit, "and Goodey Corey you be a turnning of it." When Mercy Lewis, age 19, a servant in Thomas Putnam's house, struck at the roasting scene with a stick, Ann described how Martha's apparition beat Mercy with an iron rod. Both girls shook with pain, and the family told "goodey Cory to be gone."

Within days the cries against Martha Corey rippled wide like water from cast stones. Mercy Lewis claimed her torture continued at the hands of Martha's specter. The girl charged unseen forces had dragged her helplessly across the floor toward the hearth's burning fire.

Elizabeth Hubbard, another teenaged servant, also accused Martha. Like Mercy Lewis, Elizabeth claimed that Martha's apparition bit, pinched, and choked her and urged her to write in Satan's red book. Elizabeth said she'd actually seen Martha's apparition torture Ann Putnam and her cousin Mary Walcott, as well as Mercy Lewis. Both Mercy and Elizabeth reviled Martha as a most dreadful witch. Ann Carr Putnam, young Ann's mother, also accused Martha of dreadful tortures and hellish temptations, including signing Satan's book.

Martha Corey became the fourth woman Abigail Williams accused of witchcraft. The girl divulged how Martha's apparition tortured her like the other victims. Most damning, Abigail insisted she'd seen Martha consort with the devil and take his sacrament. Eventually Martha's accusers included four married women: Mrs. Pope, Mrs. Putnam, Goodwife Bibber, and an old woman called Goodall. The three teenage girls—Mary Walcott, Mercy Lewis, and Elizabeth Hubbard—added their voices to the chorus of accusations. And the youngest accusers, aged 9 to 12, were Elizabeth Parris, Abigail Williams, and Ann Putnam. They named other women as witches, as well.

Just two days after her arrest, Martha Corey appeared before the magistrates of Salem Village. Spectators seeking entertainment thronged the meetinghouse to hear Martha's examination on March 21, a Monday. This examination could lead to an official indictment and trial for practicing witchcraft. There was no presumption of Martha's innocence. The first words from Magistrate John Hathorne accused her: "You are now in the hands of Authority tell me now why you hurt these persons."

Martha denied she'd hurt anyone and asked several times if she might pray. "We do not send for you to go to prayer," Hathorne admonished her, "But tell me why you hurt these."

"I am an innocent person: I never had to do with Witchcraft since I was born," answered Martha. "I am a Gospel Woman."

The judge pressed Martha—Who hurts these children? She must tell what she knew. Martha repeated that she was a gospel woman, "& do you think I can have to do with witchcraft too?"

How did Martha know, asked Hathorne, that the child Ann Putnam was told to observe the clothes Martha wore? Ezekiel Cheever interrupted Martha and warned her to "not begin with a lye."

Martha said she knew the children had described what the other accused women had worn. Her husband, Giles, had told her. Giles, when asked, denied he'd told this to Martha. The judge accused Martha of lying and asked her in rapid succession what she knew, who had told her about the clothes. Was it her husband or not?

"I had heard speech that the children said I trouble them," Martha finally answered, "and I thought that they might come to examine [the clothes]."

The badgering continued—"Who told you what they came for?" demanded Hathorne.

Suddenly Abigail Williams spoke up, and all eyes focused on the child pointing toward Martha. "There is a man whispering in her ear."

"What did he say to you?" Hathorne turned on Martha.

Standing before the court, her heart likely pounding against her ribs, Martha must have wondered how the children could be so confused and disoriented. "We must not believe all that these distracted children say," she told Hathorne. "I saw no body."

"But did not you hear?" asked the court.

The court records show "here was Extream agony of all the afflicted." The girls fell to the floor, writhing and shrieking in pain. Martha must have looked on, helpless and horrified.

Hathorne urged her to confess, adding, "Do you think to find mercy by aggravating your sins?"

Martha said simply, "But I cannot confess."

Hathorne changed course and brought up the incident at the Putnam house when Ann described Martha roasting a man on the spit. "Tell me what was that turning upon the Spit by you?"

Martha tried to defend herself. "You believe the Children that are distracted," she repeated. "I saw no spit."

"Do you not see how these afflicted do charge you?" demanded Harthorne.

"We must not believe distracted persons," was all Martha could answer.

No, Hathorne fired back, not distracted, not befuddled or confused. No, the full attention of these girls had locked upon Martha. This was a bewitchment. Only Martha, the accused witch, claimed the accusers were distracted. Then the judge tackled Martha for another statement she'd made earlier as reported by Edward Putnam—Martha had said that the magistrates' eyes had been blinded and she would open them.

They were blinded to accuse the innocent, said Martha, and once more she proclaimed her own innocence. She denied all accusations, saying, "What can I do? Many rise up against me."

She could start by confessing, said Hathorne.

Martha defended herself. "So I would if I were guilty."

"Now tell me the truth, will you," said Hathorne. "Why did you say that the Magistrates & Ministers eyes are blinded you would open them."

Martha laughed and denied it.

"Tell us who hurts these: We came to be a Terror to evil doers," proclaimed Hathorne.

"I have nothing to do with witchcraft," Martha repeated.

Hathorne returned to the spit-roasting incident. With what did she strike the maid at Mr. Thomas Putnam's? he asked.

"I never struck her in my life," answered Martha.

"Do you believe these children are bewitcht?"

"They may for ought I know," answered Martha. "I have no hand in it."

Martha's laughter at some of the questions provoked Hathorne to ask if she thought this "a laughing matter."

Martha denied it, but, "Ye are all against me & I cannot help it," she cried.

"Do not you believe there are Witches in the Countrey?" asked Harthorne.

"I do not know that there is any," Martha answered.

"Do not you know that Tituba Confessed it?" pushed Harthorne.

"I did not hear her speak," said Martha.

Now the court noted that when Martha made any action, the bewitched girls suffered. The Reverend Deodat Lawson, an eyewitness to Martha's examination, described how Martha's movements affected the accusers. "It was observed several times that if she did but bite her underlip in time of examination, the persons afflicted were bitten on their arms and wrists and produced the marks before the magistrates, ministers, and others." When Martha's hands were free, the girls declared she pinched them. When the court restrained Martha's hands, the girls felt no pinching. Mrs. Pope complained of "grievous torment in her bowels" when Martha "did but lean her breast against the seat in the meeting house (being the bar at which she stood)." The woman threw her muff at Martha and when that missed, threw her shoe "and hit Goodwife Corey on the head with it."

"What do you say to all these things that are apparent?" asked Hathorne, alluding to the biting and pinching tests.

"If you will all go hang me how can I help it?" asked Martha.

"Were you to serve the Devil ten years tell how many?"

Martha laughed once more, a laugh born perhaps of bitter hopelessness, of rising hysteria, as she faced the meetinghouse packed with a hundred accusing faces, the girls accusing, the magistrate accusing.

The girls suddenly cried out—Look! a yellow bird had appeared on Martha's hand. When Hathorne questioned Martha about this bird, her familiar, again she laughed. Martha denied any knowledge about a bird.

Hathorne pressed her to tell "how the Devil comes in your shape & hurts these."

"How can I know," said Martha. She must have sounded weary, maybe defeated by now.

"What book is it that you would have these children write in?"

"What book," said Martha, "were should I have a book? I showed them none, nor have none, nor brought none."

With another cry, Abigail Williams and Mary Walcott told the throng that the black man again whispered in Martha's ear. Surely, this was the devil come to advise his cohort.

The girls questioned Martha, demanding to know why she didn't join the company of witches—23 or 24 strong—gathering outside the meetinghouse? Didn't she hear the tolling drumbeat calling her to come? A shiver of fear must have swept the meetinghouse, a rising panic, that witches marshaled their forces outside God's place of worship. The accusers had ruled the day, interrupting the court, changing the course of questioning, stomping, screaming, and pitching their fits of bewitchment.

"Who is your God?" Hathorne asked Martha.

"The God that made me," answered Martha.

"What is his name?"

"Jehova," said Martha, also "God Almighty."

"Why did you say if you were a Witch you should have no pardon?"

"Because I am a [word missing] Woman," said Martha.

The court felt there'd been evidence enough of witchcraft and ordered Martha Corey taken to jail to await official trial. She joined five others accused of practicing witchcraft against Ann Putnam, Abigail Williams, Elizabeth Hubbard, and "others of Salem Village." As Martha waited in prison, the magistrates collected witnesses' depositions detailing Martha's use of witchcraft, repeating many of the charges from her March examination as well as the events from that day—how she harmed the accusers even while standing at the bar.

Giles Corey's deposition, given after Martha's examination, offered a strange mix of events easily construed as witchcraft. While sitting by the fire, he said, Martha had asked him to go

166 DAUGHTERS OF EVE

to bed, but when Giles prepared to pray, "I could nott utter my desires w'th any sense, not open my mouth to speake." Martha saw this and came to him and then he could pray. And how odd, that another time he couldn't yoke his ox for the animal sat on its haunches and wouldn't get up. Also, his cat took sick. Most telling, Giles described how Martha sat up after he went to bed. He saw her kneel on the hearth as if to pray, but heard nothing.

The first week of August a grand jury indicted Martha for using "Destestable Arts called Witchcrafts & sorceries." Martha's official trial began September 8, where she faced the testimony of Edward Putnam and Ezekiel Cheever about their visit to her on that long-ago March afternoon and how afterward she tortured members of the Putnam household. She also faced the accusations of confessors, other people themselves accused of witchcraft, who claimed Martha had joined them as a participant in the devil's work. Not surprisingly, the court found Martha guilty and sentenced her to death by hanging.

Martha Corey maintained her innocence to the end. Unlike some, she never confessed, grasping at that slim chance to save herself. She never named others as witches. On Thursday, September 22, Martha and seven more convicted of practicing witchcraft climbed into a wooden cart that drove them to the gallows. At some point on the journey the cart stuck in the mud, leaving accusers and observers wondering if "the Devil hindered it." When they reached the gallows, Martha climbed a ladder and felt the noose slip around her neck. A witness noted that Goody Corey died after saying "an Eminent Prayer upon the Ladder."

7

❦❦❦

✒A Changing World

"I wrote my father a very long letter on his plantation affairs."
    —*Eliza Lucas, manager of her family's plantations in South Carolina, July 1740*

IN THE EARLIEST DAYS of Jamestown and Plymouth, a few hundred people had struggled to survive. Only a century later, colonial citizens filled scores of villages, towns, and even a few thriving cities. An ever-growing network of dirt roads wrested from the forests linked people and places, while the ocean, rivers, and streams remained the chief highways for travelers. As Eliza Lucas noted, "We are 17 miles by land, and 6 by water from Charles Town [Charleston, South Carolina]."

"AS WELL AS MOST MEN"

As the Atlantic coast grew more settled, the rough frontier crept steadily westward, into the forests, into the mountains. Life here remained harsh and often lonely. A woman's days mirrored those of her 17th-century grandmother as she relied on herself to meet her family's needs. She hoed and harvested and shouldered a gun when necessary. William Byrd described a frontier woman in 1710: "She is a very civil woman and shews nothing of ruggedness, or Immodesty in her carriage, yett she will . . . perform the most manfull Exercises as well as most men in those parts."

The frontier wife typically lived in one room, affording little privacy. Her clothes were simple and few. Her family ate their meals off wooden dishes they shared. Young George Washington bunked with a frontier family while on a surveying mission in 1748. "I lay down before the fire upon a little hay . . . with man, wife, and children, like a parcel of dogs and cats," he wrote, "and happy is he, who gets the berth nearest the fire."

Frontier women also faced the brunt of warfare between the colonists and Native Americans. In New England, many women were taken captive for ransom money or adopted as new members into the tribe. Some white women, especially younger women, adapted to Native American life and joined the tribe. "With them [the Seneca] was my home," Mary Jemison explained to a minister.

Other women fought back, defending their homes or turning on their captors. On March 15, 1697, "The Indians fell upon some part of Haverhill [Massachusetts] about seven in the morning," recorded a New Hampshire minister. The Native Americans, members of the Abenaki tribe, "killed or carried away thirty-nine or forty persons." Hannah Duston had given birth to a baby girl, her 12th child, only a week before the attack. The Abenaki dragged Hannah and Mary Neff, a neighbor who'd been caring for Hannah, from the home. Hannah watched helplessly as an Abenaki warrior swung her newborn's head into a tree, killing the baby.

The Abenaki marched the two women 100 miles through the wilderness toward Canada. According to Duston family lore, the warriors taunted the women with visions of how they'd be stripped and forced to run the gauntlet, or tied to poles and tormented while the tribe decided their fate. Hannah determined to escape. Before dawn on March 30, 1697, she found several hatchets, and—helped by Mary and a young English boy captured earlier—Hannah, in a bloodlust of revenge, killed her captors, including three women and seven children, as they slept.

Hannah made her way back to Haverhill with 10 Native American scalps. The Massachusetts legislature granted her £25 for each trophy while Boston pulpits rang with Hannah's praises, comparing her to Biblical heroines.

"THE ENGLISH HAVE TAKEN"

Disease. Warfare. Loss of tribal lands. The invasion of several million Europeans had devastating consequences for Native American people. "The English have taken away great parts of their Country," wrote Robert Beverley in 1705. Colonists had "introduc'd drunkeness and Luxury amongst them." And Native Americans now yearned for European goods and weapons, "disiring a thousand things they never dreamt of before."

At first, Native Americans couldn't believe a European would trade 20 gleaming butcher knives for one beaver skin. "The English have no sense," said one man. Many fur traders improved business by taking Native American wives. A wife maintained friendly relations between her husband and her people. She also served as an interpreter, and, most important, she knew how to dress a skin. "Moreover," remarked Carolina trader John Lawson, "such a Man gets a great Trade with the savages."

In early fall, traders advanced the native hunters guns, ammunition, and food for the winter hunt. In summer, a hunter delivered the pelts and had his debt marked paid. Any extra income purchased more English goods: knives and hatchets, brightly colored wool fabrics, copper kettles, and jewelry.

Native Americans played the European powers against one another, trading with the French, Dutch, Spanish, or English, depending on who offered most. But Native Americans lost this leverage when the English drove the Dutch out of New York in the late 1660s and the French out of Canada in 1763.

As time passed, with millions of beaver, otter, fox, and deer skins traded, tribes fought one another for control of the best fur-trapping lands. In a series of conflicts, the powerful Iroquois nearly destroyed tribes such as the Hurons and the Erie. Some tribes spent more time hunting furs than hunting food. Women devoted more and more days to dressing skins.

But as animals were slaughtered or migrated west, the fur supply dwindled. Native Americans could not provide enough furs to cancel their debts. Some tribes, in debt to the European traders and still coveting goods, handed over even more precious acres of land.

By the time of the American Revolution, only pockets of Native Americans lived where their ancestors had farmed and hunted for centuries. The governor of South Carolina noted that his colony had once "swarmed with tribes of Indians." But by 1770, "There now remain . . . nothing of them but their names within three hundred miles of our sea coast." Most tribes survived by drifting west, away from the European advance.

BUY, BUY, BUY

Immigrants arrived regularly from England, Ireland, Germany, Holland, Sweden, Scotland, and France. Colonists produced large families. Slave ships carried more Africans and West Indian slaves to America's shores. Between 1700 and 1775 the American colonies' population grew tenfold, to 2,500,000 people.

Spending cash and begging credit for staples and luxuries, this growing population improved their standard of living. Wealthy colonists ordered goods directly from agents in England. Others were not left out of the buying spree—American shops burst with English goods: china teapots, fancy foods, fabrics and trims, books, and ready-made candles and soap. Craftsmen and seamstresses copied English and French tastes in clothes, furniture, and luxury items.

An average family possessed items that only the wealthiest had enjoyed in earlier times. Middle-class colonists dined regularly with forks—a rarity even in well-to-do 17th-century homes where fingers had served just fine for eating. They ate and drank from individual plates and cups instead of sharing wooden bowls and clay mugs. They replaced benches with wooden chairs. They sipped tea, and even the poor could buy or trade for spices. The middle class owned a few books and checked their appearance daily in a mirror. Their homes might even have windows filled with glass instead of oiled cloth, as in earlier days. The great middle-class throng rose in the world.

All this buying, however, widened the gap between rich, middle class, and poor in American society. Americans wealthy from trading and planting built many-roomed mansions stuffed with costly goods. They dined at tables gleaming with china, glass, and silver. They relaxed on plump upholstered furniture, not hard wooden chairs. Clocks chimed the hour. Thick curtains decorated glass windows. Gilt-edged books lined shelves. Family portraits hung on the walls beneath carved woodwork. Reverend Jonathan Boucher wrote a friend in England that in Virginia, "so much does Their Taste run after dress that they tell me I may see . . . more brilliant assemblies [dances] than I ever c'd [could] in the North of Engl'd."

"PRETTY GENTLEWOMAN"

Society expected the wife of a prosperous man to demonstrate polished grace and manners in all she did. Her ability to run a large home and family smoothly and thriftily reflected upon her

Domestick Amusement, engraving published in London around 1760.
The Colonial Williamsburg Foundation, Museum Purchase

husband. The old one-dish pottage—or even one course—no longer sufficed. She had to set a perfect table laden with beautifully served dishes—guests judged her on every detail. Had she mastered the techniques of carving meat, learning how to

"Thigh that Woodcock" and "Wing that Quail," "Barb that Lobster" and "Splat that Pike"? And of course the gentlewoman must display taste and elegance from head to toe.

This 18th-century gentlewoman was far removed from the 17th-century wife or the frontier woman, who "rooted in the ground" and perspired in the kitchen. A nursery rhyme defined the new ideal:

> Curly locks, Curly Locks, wilt thou be mine?
> Thou shalt not wash dishes nor yet feed the swine
> But sit on a cushion and sew a fine seam
> And feed upon strawberries, sugar, and cream.

Yet even gentlewomen worked. Benjamin Franklin wrote his favorite sister Jane, a new bride, in 1727:

> I have been thinking what would be a suitable present for me to make. . . . I had almost determined on a tea table, but when I consider that the character of a good housewife was far preferrable to that of being only a pretty gentlewoman, I concluded to send you a spinning wheel.

Mary Holyoke's diary from the 1760s listed numerous household chores alongside tea parties and receptions. She washed and ironed, sewed petticoats and shirts. She planted herbs and vegetables, raised poultry, salted pork, and bottled her own wine. She also prepared supplies of candles, salmon, and "77 Pounds of butter for winter."

Only the most financially privileged women escaped most household drudgery. Women such as Eliza Lucas Pinckney or Mrs. Robert "King" Carter had an army of enslaved laborers to follow their orders in the gardens, dairy, kitchen, and home. But a wealthy woman was not idle. She managed and supervised her busy household, training slaves and servants. She plied her sewing needle in mending or decorative embroidery. She nursed the sick. She supervised her children's upbringing and education. And because of her social status, much of her efforts involved a weary round of constant social obligations and entertaining. In one year, Mrs. Carter of Nomini Hall in Virginia served guests more than 27,000 pounds of pork, 20 head of cattle, 150 gallons of Brandy, and used 550 bushels of wheat and 100 pounds of flour.

ENSLAVED AMERICANS

Much of the colonies' expanding wealth, especially in the South, rested on the backs of slaves. The numbers of enslaved people rose dramatically with each decade. By the 1770s, nearly 500,000 persons of African descent—some free, but most enslaved— lived in the colonies.

Most enslaved black women continued working in the fields. Others took on new roles as house slaves, where they made soap, dipped candles, spun thread, wove cloth, cooked, and cleaned under the eye of the mistress.

Family life changed for many black women during the 18th century. Some plantations, or farms, grew in size and the population of enslaved people increased to work the expanding fields. African American women living on these large plantations had the chance to create a real, if tenuous, sense of family for themselves. Instead of the isolation faced by women of earlier times, they now connected to a wider web of relationships: wife and husband, mother and child, daughter, sister, niece, and aunt. Slaves could not legally marry, but many enslaved couples pledged their love to one another. The slave quarters on a large plantation worked like a small village where people grew their own vegetables in small gardens, raised chickens, spent evenings together, visited, and played with their children. All this took place under the shadow of the master's whim.

Even if family members had different owners, they might live within a few miles of their kin. Daphne, born in 1736 on the plantation of Robert Tyler, lived there her entire life, bearing 10 children and working for six different masters. In 1787, Daphne still lived with four of her children and some of her grandchildren, while others lived nearby. Masters and mistresses sometimes allowed visits and messages, but slaves stole other meetings under cover of night. Some slaves ran away to join a spouse or other kin.

Masters might allow a slave mother to keep her youngest children with her. But separation remained a constant peril. At any time a child might be taken and sold to another master, or willed away as a gift. To prevent messy and emotional good-byes, which might lead to trouble, masters often sent the child away while the mother—not suspecting she'd seen her child for the last time—worked in the fields.

But some children found their way back. One 14-year-old enslaved girl named Hagar repeatedly ran away from her master and back to her parents. A runaway notice in the *Maryland Gazette* warned that Hagar was probably being hidden "in some Negro Quarter [cabin] as her father and mother Encourage her Elopements."

Uncertainty and emotional stress preyed on a slave woman's life. A master or mistress might routinely punish a slave, and as brutally as they wanted, even over trifles such as a piece of undercooked bacon. Slaves were chained, whipped, and lived in fear. The slaves of William Byrd II and his wife, Lucy, suffered when the couple quarreled. "My wife," wrote Byrd, "caused Prue to be whipped violently notwithstanding I desired it not, which provoked me to have Anaka whipped likewise who had deserved it much more." Lucy Byrd burned her slave Little Jenny with a hot iron. On another occasion William wrestled fireplace tongs away from Lucy as she beat Little Jenny with them. Other times she had Little Jenny "soundly whipped."

THE GREAT AWAKENING

The 17th century cast women as "daughters of Eve," the tempt-ress and troublemaker. This image began transforming during the 18th century. Eve was saved, preached Cotton Mather in 1713, "by being the First of them all . . . the Mother of all that Live unto God." One 1727 poem described her as "heav'nly fair, divinely beauteous Eve."

During the 1740s, a religious revival known as the Great Awakening swept the colonies. Women flocked to hear preach-ers such as George Whitefield and Jonathan Edwards, whose emotional sermons left listeners trembling, weeping, and pray-ing on their knees. "Consider the fearful danger you are in," Edwards thundered. He described cringing "sinners" hanging "by a slender thread" over the fiery pit of hell while "the devil," he warned, "stands ready."

Jonathan Edwards may have inherited his preaching gift from his mother. Esther Stoddard Edwards held regular reli-gious meetings in her home for female neighbors. Many women dated "their first permanent attention to religion from the impression here made," wrote a meeting regular.

Women served as the backbone of 18th-century churches. In some parishes they made up nearly 70 percent of the congrega-tion. For many women, religion offered a sense of self-worth. Sermons and Bible readings stressed the importance of virtues that women should strive for: humility, charity, and gentleness. Women were viewed as more devoted to religion and more spir-itual than men. Yet most men considered theology well beyond women's understanding.

African American women also found comfort in religion. Slaves mixed Christian beliefs with elements of African reli-gions, including praying to ancestors, music, dancing, and call-ing responses. Many enslaved people identified with the Bible's stories of slavery, suffering, and eventual liberation and salvation.

TOWN LIFE

Gathering for church services or revival meetings was easiest for women who lived in towns. By the 1770s, nearly 90 percent of colonists still lived on farms where fields of tobacco, grains, and orchards had replaced towering forests. But colonial towns and villages were growing centers of population. Boston boasted 13,000 citizens by 1730; New York, 8,600 people; Philadelphia, 8,000; and Charleston, about 4,500 people.

Women who lived in towns enjoyed advantages. They browsed shops lining the streets, shopping for the latest goods from England. They might purchase prepared foods and cloth. A seamstress or milliner offered town women the chance to wear the newest fashions skillfully fitted. And a town woman more easily hired other women to help with housework than her frontier sister.

Towns also offered opportunities for culture, entertainment, and up-to-date news. People donned their best clothes, doused their hair or wigs with white powder, and danced to stately minuets or heart-pounding jigs and reels. They bet on horse races and attended theaters and concerts. As English subjects, colonists set the sky ablaze with fireworks honoring royal anniversaries, weddings, and birthdays. A Maryland woman described such an occasion in 1749: "An universal Mirth and Glee reigns . . . amongst all Ranks of People . . . nothing but Jollity and Feasting goes Forward: Musick and Dancing are the everlasting Delights."

But town life also possessed a dark side. Stinking kitchen slop, horse manure, and rotting animal carcasses clogged city streets. Privies stank from every yard. Butchers, tanners, and blubber-boilers filled gutters with blood and animal parts. Rotting garbage bobbed in the harbors. Such conditions supplied perfect breeding grounds for vermin and germs and epidemic diseases. When smallpox raged through a city, the violent

The Cotillion Dance, 1771 engraving by James Caldwell, published in London. *The Colonial Williamsburg Foundation, Museum Purchase*

disease shut down markets and blocked off towns from surrounding villages.

Towns also sheltered a growing population of poor widows and children. Civic leaders hoped to "encourage Industry and the Employment of the Poor." Town officials sent these women to work and live in places like Boston's Workhouse on the Common, founded in 1735, the New York Poorhouse, set up in 1737, and Philadelphia's Bettering Home. Local officials hired out poor women as a means to prevent idleness, to bake, spin, sew, pull flax, pick apples, do laundry, and work in the fields. The women earned a pittance for their work. The government also removed children from poor mothers and bound the youngsters out to work. In general, people viewed poverty as a mark of immoral or lazy behavior. In the Brandywine Valley of Pennsylvania, a woman hired out by the government wore a red or black *P* sewn on her sleeve as punishment for being poor.

Eliza Lucas Pinckney
A Glimpse Through Her Letterbook

THE ADVANTAGES THAT Eliza Lucas enjoyed far outstripped the hopes of most girls born in 1722. Her father, a wealthy planter, educated his Antigua-born daughter in England. When the family moved to South Carolina in 1738, teenage Eliza had mastered genteel female skills in music and embroidery. But she also gained admirers for her well-read mind and her ability to converse in French as easily as English.

War between Spain and Great Britain called Eliza's father, Lieutenant Colonel George Lucas, back to Antigua. With her brothers at school in England, a frail mother, and a younger sister, 16-year-old Eliza took on the work of running George Lucas's South Carolina plantations. The family lived at Wappoo, a 600-acre farm with 20 slaves outside of Charleston. Lucas's holdings included two other plantations, a combined 4,500 more acres, each with a force of enslaved workers and overseers.

Bright and hardworking, Eliza rose to the challenge. "I have the business of 3 plantations to transact," she penned an English friend in spring 1740, "which requires much writing and more business and fatigue of other sorts than you can imagine." But, Eliza assured, "I think myself happy that I can be useful to so good a father, and by rising very early I find I can go through much business."

Eliza managed her workforce, dealt with her father's agent in England, and kept the plantations producing a steady stream of goods: tar, pitch, lime, oak staves for barrels, rice, corn, salt, cured beef and bacon, and other products to fuel the farms and sell.

The work suited her. "I own I love the vegitable world extremely," wrote Eliza of her passion for planting. She experimented with different soils and plants, introducing ginger, figs ("with design to dry and export them"), cotton, and alfalfa to her father's farms. Loving her gardens, she indulged in planting sprees that included groves of oak and cedar. The oaks, Eliza hoped, would prove valuable for shipbuilding, and she meant for two-thirds of her oaks to be used "for a charity (I'll let you know my scheme another time)," she confided to a friend.

Eliza also experimented with indigo plants, which produced a blue dye—a color all the rage in Europe. England purchased indigo from France's West Indian colonies, money Eliza felt was a loss to England. What if South Carolina's soil could produce enough indigo to meet Britain's demand? The idea that a teenager on the edge of the British Empire could compete with France seemed ridiculous. But Eliza began with seeds that her father shipped from the British West Indies, and from that first year's crop she'd collect more seeds.

It proved a slow process. "We had a fine Crop of Indigo Seed upon the ground," she wrote her father in June 1741, but "the frost took it before it was dry. I picked out the best of it and had it planted, but there is not more than a hundred bushes of it come up. . . . I make no doubt Indigo will prove a very valuable Commodity in time. . . . I am sorry we lost this season."

Over the next few years Eliza persevered with her attempts to produce indigo. Cut plants were fermented in vats of water, then mixed and beaten, a dry white powder called lime added, the liquid poured off, and the "mud" residue spread in pressing boxes. The indigo emerged as square cakes that dried to a bright blue. The process took about three weeks. Eliza's father sent an experienced dye maker to help, but the man made "a great mistery of the process . . . and threw in so large a quantity of Lime water as to spoil the colour," Eliza later recalled. The next year a new batch of West Indian seeds failed to sprout.

Not until 1744 did Eliza harvest a promising crop of indigo. Lieutenant Colonel Lucas sent another dye maker to help his daughter, and Wappoo produced "seventeen pounds of very good Indigo." She shipped six pounds to England to see if her work earned approval. An April 1745 issue of the *South-Carolina Gazette* printed part of a letter from London proclaiming Eliza's indigo had been tried against "some of the Best FRENCH" and found just as good. Once again she saved most of the crop for seed, which she generously shared with other planters. By 1754, thanks to his daughter's efforts, George Lucas earned a tidy income from his indigo investment, and South Carolina had a new cash crop second only to rice.

Eliza's busy schedule included other pursuits. She rose at five o'clock each morning and studied till seven, when she walked the gardens or fields and saw Wappoo's slaves "are at their respective business." After breakfast she practiced music, worked on her French, and taught herself shorthand. She instructed her younger sister "and two black girls who I teach to read, and if I have my paps's approbation (my Mamas I have got) I intend [them] for school mistres's for the rest of the Negroe children—another scheme you see," she wrote friend Mary Bartlett.

Sewing occupied a portion of most days, and she even ventured to make a shrimp net, which "requires nither Eyes nor genius—at least not very good ones." Nothing seemed beyond Eliza's abilities. Several times, when a neighbor lay dangerously ill, 20-year-old Eliza stepped in and drew up their wills. She studied the legal forms in law books and made sure three people, in the company of one another, witnessed the documents. "But after all what can I do if a poor creature lies a dying and their family takes it in to their head that I can serve them. I can't refuse; but when they are well and able to employ a lawyer," she urged them to seek legal counsel instead of herself.

Penning lengthy business letters devoured hours, and Eliza also devoted time to writing friends and family, especially her father and brothers so far from home. When writing her brothers, Eliza remembered her position as a female and apologized for presuming to advise them. That didn't stop her, however, from warning them against "youthful company, pleasure, and dissipation." Months usually stretched between her letters and any replies, and worry for her loved ones proved a constant thorn.

A few times Eliza's writing flowed into the realm of poetry. Once, moved by the song of a mockingbird, she wrote Mary Bartlett, "I produced the 3 following lines while I was laceing my stays (corset)."

Sing on thou charming mimick of the feathered kind
And let the rational a lesson learn from thee,
To Mimick (not defects) but harmony.

She finished her note: "If you let any mortal besides your self see this exquisite piece of poetry, you shall never have a line more than this specimen," though how great a loss that would be she left for her friend Mary to judge.

Visiting neighbors and enjoying company in Charleston relieved Eliza's rounds of work. Mary Bartlett's aunt and uncle, Elizabeth and Charles Pinckney, often took Eliza under their wing. The Pinckneys recommended books Eliza should read and listened to her plans and schemes. In a letter to Mary, Eliza imagined what the older Pinckneys said about her oak tree plan. "'She is [a] good girl,' says Mrs. Pinckney. 'She is never Idle and always means well.' 'Tell the little Visionary,' says your Uncle, 'come to town and partake of some of the amusements suitable to her time of life.'" In another letter Eliza wrote to Mary, "Your good Uncle I know has long thought I have a fertile brain at schemeing." But Eliza did not see her schemes as mere whims, and felt that "Out of many surely one may hit."

A wealthy and accomplished young woman like Eliza attracted male admirers. George Lucas, who rose to lieutenant governor of Antigua, passed on the names of two gentlemen interested in marrying her. In her 1740 reply Eliza professed obedience to her father, but she asks him to thank "the old Gentleman for his Generosity and favourable sentiments of me." However, "the riches of Peru and Chili if he had them put together could not purchase a sufficient Esteem for him to make him my husband." She didn't know the other suitor well enough to even judge him. Eliza assured her father she enjoyed the single life and, "as I am yet but Eighteen, hope you will [put] aside the thoughts of my marrying yet these 2 or 3 years at least."

But Eliza did marry, as was her duty. In a few short months during 1743 and 1744 her life changed. Family finances had taken a hit. Like most planters, her father had land but little money, and Wappoo and his other properties were mortgaged to the hilt. Eliza rented out Wappoo—keeping hold of the fields growing her indigo crop—and prepared to return to Antigua with her sister and mother.

But in January 1744 her friend Elizabeth Pinckney died after a long illness. Four months later, on May 27, 22-year-old Eliza married the widower, her mentor and friend Charles Pinckney, age 45. Such quick marriages were a staple of colonial America. The couple knew each other well, and the marriage proved a happy one. Over the next six years Eliza bore four children, Charles Cotesworth (born 1746), George Lucas (born and died in 1747), a daughter named Harriott (born 1748), and another son Thomas (born in 1750).

Eliza married into a world similar to the one she'd grown up in, a world of land and plantations, a home in Charleston, and the labor of that world borne on the backs of enslaved African Americans. As a married woman, Eliza turned her considerable energies toward her husband and children, though never abandoning her passions for plants and schemes. She tried her hand at raising mulberry trees and silkworms, which never turned into a prosperous business like her indigo efforts did.

In 1753 the Pinckneys sailed to England, the heart of the empire and the place Charles and Eliza wanted their sons educated. They enjoyed sightseeing at Stonehenge, Salisbury Cathedral, and Bath before the boys settled into school and Charles settled into his job as South Carolina's representative to the Board of Trade in London. Eliza loved the social whirl of London— visiting museums and attending the theater and music recitals. "I hope Mr. P. will be quite reconciled to England for the time he proposes to stay here," she confided to a friend. "At present he is not quite satisfied with it and has many [y]earnings after his native land."

After nearly five years, and with war now raging between France and Britain, Charles determined to return to South Carolina long enough to tend his businesses there. Eliza suffered at the thought of leaving her sons behind for two or three years, "and considering the uncertainty of life, perhaps for ever!" she wrote Lady Carew, a friend from Eliza's own school days in England. The world seemed in turmoil, and Eliza poured out her heart, how four years before they'd left South Carolina a flourishing colony, valuable to Great Britain. They would never have had the "least doubt of its being protected and taken care of in case of a war, tho a War then seemed a very distant contingency. . . . But how much reason we have had to change our sentiments," she wrote.

Within three weeks of their return to South Carolina, in May 1758, Eliza's world crashed to bits—Charles caught a malarial

A gold-colored gown Eliza Pinckney had made in England from silk
she'd manufactured in South Carolina.

Division of Home and Community Life, National Museum of American History,
Smithsonian Institution

fever and died suddenly. Stricken with grief and shock, Eliza could not even write her sons the news of their father's death for over a month.

> Let it be a comfort to you, my dear babes, as long as you live that you had such a father! He has set you a great and good example. . . . His affection for you was as great as ever was upon Earth! And you were good children and deserved it. He thought you so; he blessed and thanked God for you. . . . We must drink of the cup it has pleased God to Give us, a bitter Cup indeed!

Eliza pledged, "All my future life may be spent to do you good, and in showing to you, the dear pledges of sincerest affection that ever was upon Earth, how much, how truly, I loved and honoured Your dear father."

Eliza's grief and depression lengthened like a dark shadow. To Lady Carew she wrote a year later, "My Nights have passed in tears and days in sighs since . . . I was deprived of what my soul held most dear upon Earth." She struggled to carry on, to get down to the business of running the Pinckney properties and plantations. In March 1760, Eliza wrote her business agent in London that hard work kept her busy.

> Had there not been a necessity for it, I might have sunk to the grave by this time in that Lethargy of stupidity which had seized me. . . . But a variety of imployment gives my thoughts a relief from melloncholy subjects, tho' 'tis but a temporary one, and gives me air and exercise, which I believe I should not have had resolution enough to take if I had not been roused to it by motives of duty and parental affection.

Eliza never remarried but devoted her energies to her children and their legacies. Barrels of ink flowed from her pen in long letters of advice for her sons and their caregivers. "Be good children," she admonished, "mind your learning and love one another." She especially worried about Charles Cotesworth, on the brink of young manhood, "in a City surrounded with temptations with every youthful passion about you." Keep vigilant, she warned, and always check his temper; when unleashed it brought "the greatest mischiefs and misfortunes." A few months later, perhaps remembering her own burdens as a teenager, Eliza wrote Charles Cotesworth that, though young, "the welfair of a whole family depends in a great measure on the progress you make in moral Virtue, Religion, and learning." Raising her sons at such a distance proved hard for Eliza, and she did not see her boys again until they were grown men in their early 20s.

But the children did well. Harriott Pinckney married a rice planter at age 19, and Eliza often visited at her daughter's home. Charles Cotesworth and Thomas fought for the United States in the Revolutionary War—which devastated much of the Pinckney estates—and later served in South Carolina and national government. Eliza remained a vibrant woman until her death from cancer on May 26, 1793. She had traveled to Philadelphia, the new nation's capitol, seeking medical treatment. President George Washington, who'd met Eliza during his 1791 tour of the South, requested to serve as a pallbearer.

Eliza Lucas Pinckney's *Letterbook* offers a glimpse of a curious, energetic woman who expected much of herself and those around her. She followed her duty, as befit a woman of colonial America and later, the new nation. "No time is ours but the present—and that so fleeting that we can hardly be said to exist," she wrote as a teenager. Yet Eliza made the most of her days, she left her mark, her children did her proud, and her work with indigo is still remembered today.

Eve, and Others, Belonging to the Randolphs

PEYTON RANDOLPH SERVED the colony of Virginia well. He held many positions including attorney general and Speaker of the House of Burgesses. Then, turning his back on the crown, he helped lead the revolutionary movement in Virginia. He presided as president at the First Continental Congress in 1774 and served as a delegate to the Second Continental Congress. Peyton Randolph died in Philadelphia of an "apoplectic stroke" on October 23, 1775, months before Congress adopted the Declaration of Independence written by Peyton's young cousin, Thomas Jefferson.

As the white male delegates from 13 colonies gathered to discuss how Great Britain had enslaved them and trampled their rights, Randolph's will was read. He left his estate, including his house and outbuildings in Williamsburg, his furniture, horses, and chariot, to his beloved wife, Betty. He also bequeathed other important property to his wife: "Little Aggy & her children, Great Aggy & her children, Eve & her children Lucy & her children to her & her heirs forever."

Like thousands of other enslaved women, Aggy, Eve, and Lucy appear as names in a will, not as people but as property, women and children who left behind little historical record to flesh out their stories. Aggy, Eve, and others may have become Peyton Randolph's property when he wed Elizabeth "Betty" Harrison on March, 8, 1745. Betty Harrison had been raised at Berkeley, a grand James River plantation, and both Betty's parents—Ann Carter and Benjamin Harrison—belonged to Virginia's most prestigious families.

Betty and Peyton had no children, but they took great interest in their nieces and nephews. Young relatives often resided in the Randolph home's extra bedchambers. As politics and public duties consumed her husband's time, Betty Randolph ran their properties, including three plantations, and kept accounts from her own office in the Williamsburg home. With their lofty position in the capital, the Randolphs entertained lavishly. Betty Randolph presided over dinner parties five or more evenings a week, each meal at least four courses, the table settings—down to the pressed tablecloth—changed between each course.

Betty Randolph herself did not cook, serve, clear, or wash dishes for these elaborate dinners. Twenty-seven slaves, including Eve, Great Aggy, Lucy, Charlotte, and an enslaved woman also named Betty, worked under her command and her watchful eye. Where a field slave on the plantation might have Sunday off and a chance to occasionally avoid the master's gaze, town slaves were always under scrutiny and on call 24 hours a day, seven days a week.

Most town slaves were women and children. A man might drive a carriage or serve as butler or footman, but women did most of the work in the Randolph household—the cooking, laundry, dairy work, weaving, spinning, cleaning, and serving. Living and working closely with the white family, these women would have known all the news of Virginia's capital. The five to seven slaves who poured wine and whisked away the plates at

Mrs. Randolph's dinner parties overheard every political discussion and knew every rumor as the rift widened between Great Britain and her colonies.

An inventory taken after Peyton Randolph's death showed that two women, Eve and Betty, were some of the most valuable slaves he owned. Valued at £100 each, this hefty sum spoke to the women's training and skills. Aggy, who probably washed and ironed, had a value of £60; while an older woman, good for watching children while their mothers worked, had a value of only £10.

Betty may have been the Randolphs' cook, an indispensable woman who probably lived above the brick-floored kitchen and had a few other slave women or children to help her. Betty would have worked long days, beginning before daylight as she rekindled the fire, fetched water, and put the kettle on to boil. She might also have been in charge of feeding chickens or milking cows. Morning chores included baking bread and cooking breakfast for the family and enslaved workers.

After breakfast Mrs. Randolph probably arrived in the kitchen. She gave orders for dinner, read out recipes, and measured ingredients, many of them kept under lock and key so her slaves couldn't steal food. Twice a week Betty accompanied Mrs. Randolph to the open-air market for meat and fresh produce, a chance to escape the kitchen and feel part of the town. Perhaps she spoke to other slaves, taking part in a thriving web of information.

A line of servants carried the dinner Betty created to the dining room in mid-afternoon. This was the main meal of the day. Later, around eight o'clock in the evening, she prepared supper, a lighter meal than the courses served earlier in the day. At night Betty cleaned up, mixed the next day's bread, prepared a pot of hominy for the slaves' breakfast, and banked the kitchen fire to rekindle the following morning. Only after this day was finished could Betty claim time with her family.

Depending on the season, Betty may also have preserved food, made soap, roasted coffee beans, brewed small beer, and helped with mending and other chores. As a cook, Betty gained certain benefits, including the chance to eat leftover food. She might earn hand-me-down clothes and items cast off from Mrs. Randolph or her nieces.

Like Betty, highly valued Eve held a position of note among the Randolph slaves. Most likely, Eve worked as Mrs. Randolph's personal maid. Everything in Mrs. Randolph's considerable knowledge of running a household, she trained Eve to do. Eve was on call whenever Mrs. Randolph needed her and likely slept on a mattress outside the Randolph's bedroom door, maybe even in the bedroom itself.

Each morning Eve rose before her mistress, readied the fire, and warmed the bedchamber. She laid out Mrs. Randolph's shift, stockings, stays, petticoats, and gown, and helped her mistress dress. Eve relayed Mrs. Randolph's instructions to the other household slaves. She mended Mrs. Randolph's clothes and ran errands. At night she warmed the bedsheets and helped undress and prepare her mistress for bed. Eve's round-the-clock duties spared little time for her own son, George, even though they both lived on the Randolphs' Williamsburg property. Eve finally lay down to sleep after Betty Randolph retired.

If Mrs. Randolph believed her enslaved women content, even happy, with their lives, she must have been shaken as matters turned in the month following her husband's death. As British authority crumbled in towns and villages, many of the royal governors fled, including Virginia's royal governor, John Murray, Lord Dunmore. The governor and his family abandoned the capital of Williamsburg for the safety of a British warship in the Chesapeake Bay.

Before he fled, Dunmore issued a proclamation on November 7, 1775, that sent shock waves through the colony. He promised freedom to any indentured servants and slaves who deserted

By his Excellency the Right Honourable JOHN Earl of DUNMORE, his Majesty's Lieutenant and Governour-General of the Colony and Dominion of Virginia, and Vice-Admiral of the fame:

A PROCLAMATION.

AS I have ever entertained Hopes that an Accommodation might have taken Place between *Great Britain* and this Colony, without being compelled, by my Duty, to this moſt diſagreeable, but now abſolutely neceſſary Step, rendered ſo by a Body of armed Men, unlawfully aſſembled, firing on his Majeſty's Tenders, and the Formation of an Army, and that Army now on their March to attack his Majeſty's Troops, and deſtroy the well-diſpoſed Subjects of this Colony: To defeat ſuch treaſonable Purpoſes, and that all ſuch Traitors, and their Abetters, may be brought to Juſtice, and that the Peace and good Order of this Colony may be again reſtored, which the ordinary Courſe of the civil Law is unable to effect, I have thought fit to iſſue this my Proclamation, hereby declaring, that until the aforeſaid good Purpoſes can be obtained, I do, in Virtue of the Power and Authority to me given, by his Majeſty, determine to execute martial Law, and cauſe the ſame to be executed throughout this Colony; and to the End that Peace and good Order may the ſooner be reſtored, I do require every Perſon capable of bearing Arms to reſort to his Majeſty's S T A N-DARD, or be looked upon as Traitors to his Majeſty's Crown and Government, and thereby become liable to the Penalty the Law inflicts upon ſuch Offences, ſuch as Forfeiture of Life, Confiſcation of Lands, &c. &c. And I do hereby farther declare all indented Servants, Negroes, or others (appertaining to Rebels) free, that are able and willing to bear Arms, they joining his Majeſty's Troops, as ſoon as may be, for the more ſpeedily reducing this Colony to a proper Senſe of their Duty, to his Majeſty's Crown and Dignity.   I do farther order, and require, all his Majeſty's liege Subjects to retain their Quitrents, or any other Taxes due, or that may become due, in their own Cuſtody, till ſuch Time as Peace may be again reſtored to this at preſent moſt unhappy Country, or demanded of them for their former ſalutary Purpoſes, by Officers properly authoriſed to receive the ſame.

GIVEN under my Hand, on Board the Ship William, off Norfolk, the 7th Day of November, in the 16th Year of his Majeſty's Reign.

D U N M O R E.

G O D   SAVE   THE   K I N G.

Lord Dunmore's Proclamation that encouraged Eve and other Randolph slaves to run away. *Virginia Memory, Library of Virginia* rebellious masters and who "are able and willing to bear Arms, they joining His Majesty's Troops." Dunmore needed soldiers. Rebel leaders cried this was an excuse to steal the slave labor of patriots, while Dunmore and other loyalists kept their own slaves. A letter published in the *Virginia Gazette* on November 24 pointed out that Dunmore had no use for "the aged, the infirm, the women and children, [who] are still to remain the property of their masters."

Thousands of Virginia's enslaved—including women in the Randolph household—saw this as a rare chance for freedom, and any chance, no matter how slim, must be grasped. Eight slaves ran from the Randolph house, including Aggy, Eve, and Lucy. But by July 1776, four had returned, either caught and taken back to Mrs. Randolph or forced to return by an outbreak of smallpox in Dunmore's crowded camp that killed hundreds of runaway slaves.

In June 1780, Mrs. Randolph wrote her will, mixing gifts of prized possessions with her human possessions. Once more, as in Peyton Randolph's will, the names of their slaves appeared on the list of property distributed and dispersed on their owner's death.

I give to my Nephew Benjamin Harrison of Berkley four Silver Candlesticks called the new ones which were given me by my grandmother Harrison I also give him a mulatto [biracial] Woman called little Aggy, her Daughter Betsy and her son Nathan to him and his heirs forever. I also give him the other half of the Beds Blankets and Curtains. . . . I give to my niece Ann Coupland a Negro woman named Eve and her son George to her use and after her death to her Heirs. I give to my niece Elizabeth Rickman a Negro woman called great Aggy and her son Henry to her use and after her death to her Heirs. I give to my Niece Lucy Randolph . . . a molatto

girl named Charlotte to her use and after her death to her
Heirs. I give to my Nephew Harrison Randolph a negro
woman named Lucy and her Children to him and his
Heirs forever.

It must have seemed a cruel joke to Eve and the others that a
war fought for liberty left slaves in bondage. A little more than a
year after Mrs. Randolph wrote her will, in the autumn of 1781,
Eve ran away again with her 15-year-old son, George. They fled
to British general Lord Charles Cornwallis's forces at Yorktown,
only a few miles from Williamsburg. There, George Washington's soldiers, with the aid of French troops and ships, defeated
Cornwallis.

As British supplies dwindled during the siege of Yorktown,
the Redcoats drove the runaway slaves out from behind British
lines. Starving and sick with smallpox, they died in great numbers. Thomas Jefferson estimated about 30,000 Virginia slaves
had run to Cornwallis, "and that of these about 27,000 died of
the small pox and camp fever."

George may have been one of those who died. He is not men-
tioned in the advertisement Mrs. Randolph's nephew posted in
the *Virginia Gazette or American Advertiser* on February 2, 1782.

TWENTY DOLLARS REWARD, FOR apprehending
EVE, a Negro woman slave, who left York after the sur-
render; she is about forty years old, very black and slender, has a small mouth for a Negro, and a remarkable
mole on her nose: She has since been seen on her way to
Hampton. She carried with her a variety of striped and
checked Virginia cloth cloathes. Whoever delivers her
to the subscriber in Richmond, shall receive the above
reward. HARRISON RANDOLPH.

At some point Eve was caught and returned to Mrs. Randolph. Between the February 1782 runaway advertisement and July 20, 1782, Mrs. Randolph sold Eve. On that July date she penned a codicil (amendment) to her will: "Whereas Eve's bad behaviour laid me under the necessity of selling her. I order and direct the money she sold for may be laid out in purchasing two negroes Viz, a Boy & Girl, the Girl I give to my niece Ann Copland in lieu of Eve, in the same manner that I had given Eve."

Elizabeth "Betty" Randolph died on January 31, 1783. Her death must have unleashed a rush of fear and panic through her enslaved people. According to Mrs. Randolph's will, along with her silver candlesticks, the beds, and the curtains, each slave would go to a new home. Each enslaved woman would have to adjust to the demands, rules, whims, and punishments of a new master and mistress. If they felt any blessing in Mrs. Randolph's will it must have been the fact that each woman remained with her children. At least for the moment.

Christiana Campbell
& Jane Vobe
Keeping a Busy Tavern

CHRISTIANA BURDETT GREW up in a tavern-keeping family. Like most colonial children, from a young age she must have helped her parents, John and Mary, at the family's Williamsburg Virginia tavern, also known as an ordinary or public house. In 1746 Christiana's father died, leaving her £300 and three slaves—Shropshire, Bell, and Bell's child. Even though she was a 24-year-old single female, an unlikely person for the courts to trust with legal and financial decisions, Christiana qualified as executor of her father's estate.

Christiana was not a young woman by colonial standards when she settled her father's affairs. A few months after his death she married an apothecary named Ebenezer Campbell on September 19, 1746. The newlyweds set up business in Blandford, Virginia. Around 1750 Christiana gave birth to a daughter named Mary, though the family called the baby Molly, a common nickname.

In 1752 Christiana was once again pregnant. But before the baby arrived tragedy struck the little family when Ebenezer died. Suddenly a widow, Christiana gave birth to a second daughter and named her "Ebe" after her father. On August 14, 1752, the administrators of Ebenezer's estate advertised an auction of all his medicines and medical instruments, his library, his personal property and furniture, his horses, and apothecary shop. On her own now with two young children to support, Christiana returned to the capital city of Williamsburg. Church records show she was living there by October 1753, when she had a young slave, named London, baptized at Williamsburg's Bruton Parish Church.

Millinery and tavern keeping were the most profitable employments for a woman, and Christiana already had experience running and working a tavern. Christiana rented several properties over the next decade and probably served food and drink and rented rooms at those locations. Records from 1755 offer proof she fed a host of patrons, for she ordered large amounts of food including 25 bushels of wheat and 111 pounds of beef.

In the fall of 1771, using a legacy bequeathed her by her landlord, and possibly with further aid from financial backers, Christiana purchased a tavern. The building had at least eight rooms and two covered porches. This tavern, previously run by another woman innkeeper named Jane Vobe, had a choice location across from the capitol building where the General Assembly met. It also overlooked the exchange—an open area where men transacted trade and financial business. Christiana could stand on her wide front porch and watch the movers and shakers of the colonial capital.

On October 2, 1771, the *Virginia Gazette* announced Christiana's new endeavor:

I BEG LEAVE to acquaint the Publick that I have opened TAVERN in the House, behind the Capitol, lately occupied by Mrs. Vobe; where those Gentlemen who please to favour me with their Custom may depend upon genteel Accommodations, and the very best Entertainment. I shall reserve Rooms for the Gentlemen who formerly lodged with me.

CHRISTIANNA CAMPBELL.

Jane Vobe, who had run a tavern in Williamsburg since 1752, moved to another location and established a new successful tavern that rivaled Christiana's. Located on the city's main road, she called her tavern the Sign of the King's Arms, although most people referred to the business simply as "Mrs. Vobe's." A few months after Christiana Campbell opened her new place, Jane ran her own announcement in the *Virginia Gazette*:

February 6, 1772.
I BEG Leave to acquaint my former Customers, and the Publick in General, that I have just opened Tavern opposite to the Raleigh [Tavern], at the Sign of the King's Arms, being the house lately occupied by Mr. John Carter, and shall be much obliged to the Gentlemen who favour me with their Company.

JANE VOBE.

I am in Want of a good COOK, and would be glad to hire or Purchase one.

Jane and Christiana not only ran successful businesses—businesses that catered almost exclusively to male customers—but the ladies were an even rarer commodity, women who owned property in their own names.

As the capital city, Williamsburg thrived as a hub of activity for people gathering for court sessions and meetings of the House of Burgesses. Farmers and great planters arrived to bargain, trade, and sell. Christiana Campbell and Jane Vobe served

A re-creation of Jane Vobe's tavern, built on the original foundations.
Brandon Marie Miller

the important men of the colony, including Thomas Jefferson and George Washington, in the 1760s and 1770s. In his diary, Washington recorded dining at Mrs. Campbell's ten times within a two-month span, keeping track of what he'd paid. He also "supped" often and lodged at the King's Arms. Jane Vobe and Christiana Campbell stayed in business for decades by securing customer loyalty and offering the best in food and lodging.

Christiana's daughters probably worked at their mother's place of business until they married. Running a busy tavern required much work—hands for cooking, chopping wood, washing laundry, waiting tables, and caring for visitors' horses. Both Jane and Christiana owned male and female slaves, adults and children. By 1762, records show that Christiana regularly sent her household's enslaved children to the Bray School, a Williamsburg establishment to educate black children in reading, writing, and Christianity. Girls also learned to sew and knit. One of Jane Vobe's slaves, a man named Gowan Pamphlet, became a well-known Baptist preacher.

Work began early in a tavern, hours before sunrise, around four o'clock in the morning. Christiana and Jane, accompanied by an enslaved servant, probably went to the outdoor market early to buy the best food before the city's housewives arrived. It would have been a matter of pride to serve Williamsburg's strangers and visitors a high-quality experience. Their establishments also served city residents and laborers who stopped in for a meal or a tankard of drink. Both inns had large kitchens behind the tavern buildings, as did most homes, to prevent fires, and a separate building devoted to laundry.

Much of a female tavern keeper's job was an extension of her normal role—she now cooked, served, and cared for others on a grander scale. As business owners, Christiana and Jane probably possessed at least basic skills of reading, writing, and ciphering (math) to keep accounts. Debt collection was a necessary part of doing business, and they must have known when to press or cajole a customer.

Women like Christiana and Jane not only served food and drink to customers, they also contributed to the social life of Williamsburg. All manner of gambling and card playing were popular. Christiana's and Jane's taverns must have seen their share of sporting games. A French visitor noted he "got lodgings at Mrs. Jane Vobe's tavern where all the best people resort." "There is not a publick house in Virginia," he added, "but have their tables all battered with the [dice boxes], which shews the Extravagant Disposition of the planters." Washington recorded he sometimes visited "The Club at Mrs. Campbells," which may have been a private room where gentlemen might talk and gamble into the night.

Washington, a theater lover, noted several times he'd bought "Play Tickets" from Mrs. Campbell. Did she host a performance at her tavern, or did she sell tickets for entertainment carried on at other Williamsburg venues? Tavern keepers often welcomed a variety of entertainment for their customers—traveling actors; magicians; people with physical deformities, who inspired enthusiastic gawking; and animal acts, including displays of camels, moose, and leopards.

Jane Vobe also sold theater tickets as well as raffle tickets and lottery tickets. She thought her patrons might appreciate a little art. The *Virginia Gazette* updated Williamsburg's citizens: "Mr. Pratt, a portrait painter, Lately from England and Ireland But last from New York, has brought with him to Williamsburg a small but very neat collection of paintings which are now on exhibition at Mrs. Vobes." Jane also offered her customers a garden for their pleasure. In an ad from May 1773, she notified the public: "Lost in the Garden at Mrs. Vobe's . . . a plain SILVER WATCH with a Steel Chain. . . . Whoever brings the said watch to the Bar of the said Mrs. Vobe shall have TWENTY SHILLINGS reward." Jane also earned extra income by renting out a small building on her property for a shop.

Citizens occasionally gathered at Christiana's and Jane's for dances—a popular pastime among Virginians. A dance required that ladies enter the mainly male domain of the tavern. A rival Williamsburg tavern, Wetherburn's Tavern, added a room for dancing with a separate entrance for ladies so they needn't pass through the bar. Traveling musicians toting their own fiddles and flutes supplied the tunes. Usually, the tavern keeper did not pay these men, but passed a hat for money to cover the musicians' fee. Most evenings, people enjoyed listening and singing along to romantic, storytelling ballads, bawdy songs, and funny or political tunes.

At all times, the universal colonial drink of rum flowed, a bowl of rum punch always at hand, or Flip—a strong beer sweetened with sugar or molasses and mixed with rum. At a tavern such as Christiana Campbell's or the King's Arms, customers of every class mingled in the crowded public rooms or shared sleeping quarters upstairs.

As tavern keepers running establishments busy from early morning until late at night, Jane, Christiana, and their servants must have known everything going on in the colony. In the flickering candlelight of their crowded ordinaries they listened to public debates and discussions on the issues of the day as well as juicy gossip about their neighbors. Their taverns served as meeting places for groups such as the Williamsburg Lodge of Masons and the Ohio Company of land speculators. Members of the assembly would discuss politics over drinks and food.

Christiana and Jane ran their businesses through the dangerous years of the American Revolution. Jane's tavern lodged both American and allied French officers during 1781, the year the allies fought Lord Charles Cornwallis at the Battle of Yorktown. Baron von Steuben, a Prussian general who joined the American cause, boarded at the King's Arms in March 1781, paying for lodgings and liquors, as well as stable space for his horse.

Political changes and war transformed the two women's lives. When Virginia's capital moved to Richmond in 1782 many Williamsburg businesses faltered, including Christiana Campbell's and the King's Arms. In 1783, a visitor who stopped in for Christiana's famous oysters noted Campbell no longer ran her tavern. The young Yorktown merchant rather ungraciously described Christiana as "a little old Woman about four feet high; & equally thick." Jane Vobe moved her business in 1786 across the James River from Richmond, but she continued to own her Williamsburg property. Christiana died March 25, 1792.

Christiana Campbell and Jane Vobe owned competing but successful taverns in Virginia's capital city as the colonial era rushed to an end with the American Revolution. As women of a new nation, what must they have felt when a tall, dashing former customer was elected the first president of the United States? Who'd have thought it!

8

⚜

A Tapestry of Lives

WOMEN IN COLONIAL AMERICA lived in a society defined entirely by men. People expected a woman to quietly shine with meekness, piety, obedience, and diligence. She won praise as a "worthy matron," "honored mother," "friendly neighbor," "obedient wife," and "virtuous maiden."

So many colonial women's stories, especially Native American and African American women, remain untold and unknown, never recorded and lost in the centuries since they lived. Sometimes, though, a woman's story resurfaces, offering a glimpse of how women felt about themselves and one another. Esther Edwards Burr was the daughter of famed preacher Jonathan Edwards. In April 1757 she penned a letter to a friend:

> I have had a Smart Combat with Mr. Ewing about our Sex. . . . *He did not think women knew what Friendship was. They were hardly capable of anything so cool & rational as friendship*—(My Tongue you know hangs pretty loose, . . .) I retorted several severe things unto him before he had

Elizabeth Clarke Freake (Mrs. John Freake) and Baby Mary, painted about 1671–1674. *Worcester Art Museum (Massachusetts), Gift of Mr. and Mrs. Albert W. Rice, 1963.134*

time to speak again . . . we carried on the dispute for an hour—I talked him quite silent.

Esther died in 1758 at the age of 26, but the trace of her independent spirit has endured. She would not rest while the honor of women's friendships was disputed—because she knew the value of those friendships firsthand. One of Esther's friends, Sarah Prince, described her grief at losing Esther. "My whole Prospects in this world are now Changed," Sarah wrote. "She knew and felt all my Griefs. . . . She laid out herself for my good. . . . O the tenderness which tied our hearts!"

The experiences of Native American women, black women, and white women were woven together into the fabric of colonial life. Through their labor from sunrise into darkness, they clothed and fed their families. They were strong, resourceful survivors under the harshest conditions. Women, indeed, played a part in "the better strengthening" of the colonies. Many of them paid a high price for this changing world.

Anne Bradstreet summed up much of a woman's outlook on life in 1664: "If we had no winter, the spring would not be so pleasant," she wrote, "if we did not sometimes taste of adversity, prosperity would not be so welcome."

NOTES

1: The Natural Inhabitants

"*We were entertained*": David, ed., *Hakluyt's Voyages*, 450.

"*the wife of Granganimo*": David, *Hakluyt's Voyages*, 450.

"*for a more kinde and loving*": David, *Hakluyt's Voyages*, 451.

"*In the management*": Axtell, ed., *The Indian Peoples of Eastern America: A Documentary History of the Sexes*, 92.

"*as fair a show*": Moynihan, Russet, and Crumpacker, eds., *Second to None: A Documentary History of American Women*, 25.

"*She cooks victuals regularly*": Axtell, *Indian Peoples*, 92.

"*at the very shadow*": Axtell, *Beyond 1492: Encounters in Colonial North America*, 133.

"*may then do what she*": Axtell, *Indian Peoples*, 92.

in providing for others: Axtell, *Indian Peoples*, 92.

"*Plenty of time to waste*": Axtell, *Indian Peoples*, 110.

"*I know many couples*": Moynihan, Russet, and Crumpacker, *Second to None*, 28.

"*The mother's title rests*": Moynihan, Russet, and Crumpacker, *Second to None*, 33.

"Pregnant women among them": Axtell, Indian Peoples, 8.
"are scarcely heard to groane": Moynihan, Russet, and Crumpacker, Second to None, 28.
"The [native] Women": Moynihan, Russet, and Crumpacker, Second to None, 41.
"Thou dishonorest me": Axtell, Indian Peoples, 34.

2: In This New Discovered Virginia

"In a newe plantation": Jones, American Work: Four Centuries of Black and White Labor, 39.
For more than 200 years it was assumed the 1607 Jamestown fort had vanished beneath the James River. Starting in 1994 archaeologists discovered remains of the original stockade. Today, the Jamestown Rediscovery Project is one of the top archaeological sites in the world, with more than one million artifacts already taken from the ground and foundations of early structures—like the first church—uncovered.
Most colonists considered: Jones, American Work, 23.
"Our men," wrote George Percy: Billings, Jamestown and the Founding of the Nation, 34.
"The first gentlewoman": Arber, ed., Travels and Works of Captain John Smith 1580–1631, 446.
"Great Sweating": Kupperman, "Fear of Hot Climates in the Anglo-American Experience," 221.
"his wife as she slept": Arber, ed., Travels and Works, 2: 498.
"The want of wives": Spruill, Women's Life and Work in the Southern Colonies, 8.
"for the better strengthening": Spruill, Women's Life and Work, 4.
"The Woman Outwitted": Kamensky, The Colonial Mosaic: American Women 1600–1760, 26.
"tye and roote the Planters": Ransome, "Wives for Virginia, 1621," 7.
"younge, handsome": Ransome, "Wives for Virginia," 7.
"specially recommended for their": Ransome, "Wives for Virginia," 10.
"honest and industrious Planters": Ransome, "Wives for Virginia," 7.
"They are so wild": Smith, The Generall Historie of Virginia, New England, and the Summer Isles, 1624, 71.

"penetrable For the Plough": Jones, *American Work*, 28.
"be very painful": Arber, ed., *Travels and Works* 1: 363.
"It is almost incredible": Moynihan, Russet, and Crumpacker, *Second to None*, 26.
"most deare and wel-beloved daughter": Smith, *Generall Historie*, 121.
A few years later: Berkin, *First Generations: Women in Colonial America*, 107.
But a census from 1625: Kamensky, *Colonial Mosaic*, 24; Purvis, *Almanacs of American Life: Colonial America to 1763*, 13.

Pocahontas

"dearest jewell": Smith, *The Generall Historie of Virginia, New England, and the Summer Isles, 1624*, 49
"feasted him after their": Smith, *Generall Historie*, 49.
"and laid her owne": Smith, *Generall Historie*, 49.
"Powhatan understanding we detaine": Smith, *A True Relation of Occurences and Accidents in Virginia, 1608*, 180.
"for feature, countenance, and proportion": Smith, *True Relation*, 180.
"the Kings Daughter": Smith, *True Relation*, 183.
"such trifles as contented her": Smith, *True Relation*, 183.
"a well featured, but wanton": Strachey, *Historie of Travaile into Virginia Britannia, 1612*, 65.
"I am verie hungrie": Townsend, *Pocahontas and the Powhatan Dilemma*, 73.
"What can you get by war": Townsend, *Powhatan Dilemma*, 79.
"Such things as shee delighted in": Smith, *Generall Historie*, 77.
"younge Pocohunta": Strachey, *Historie of Travaile*, 54.
"I was told . . . that the": Townsend, *Powhatan Dilemma*, 101.
"by any stratagem": Townsend, *Powhatan Dilemma*, 101
"If he did not betray": Townsend, *Powhatan Dilemma*, 102.
"Now was the greatest labor": Townsend, *Powhatan Dilemma*, 102.
"she must goe with him": Smith, *Generall Historie*, 112.
"pensive and discontented": Townsend, *Powhatan Dilemma*, 105.
"They tooke Pokahuntis prisoner": Purchas, *Purchas His Pilgrimage*.
"would have betrayed his": Reutiman, "The Forgotten Kidnapping: The Transformation of the Pocahontas Captivity Story."
"dwell with the English men": Townsend, *Powhatan Dilemma*, 120.

"such diabolical assaults": All quotes from John Rolfe taken from his letter to Governor Dale.

"She lives . . . lovingly": Townsend, *Powhatan Dilemma*, 134.

"doe runn headlong": Townsend, *Powhatan Dilemma*, 133.

"she next under God": Smith, *Generall Historie*, 121.

"Here is . . . no fayre Lady": Townsend, *Powhatan Dilemma*, 149.

"entertained her with festival": Purchas, *Purchas His Pilgrimage*, 19.

"not only accustome her selfe": Purchas, *Purchas His Pilgrimage*, 17.

"Not seeming well contented": Smith, *Generall Historie*, 123.

"You did promise Powhatan . . . your Countriemen will lie much": Smith, *Generall Historie*, 123

Cecily Jordan Farrar

"Ancient Planter": London Company's instructions to Governor Yeardley, 1619, www.encyclopediavirginia.org/_Instructions_to_George _Yeardley_by_the_Virginia_Company_of_London_November _18_1618.

Cecily Jordan Farrar is one of the author's ancestors.

"I Grivell Pooley take thee": Kingsbury, *The Records of the Virginia Company of London*, vol. 4, 219.

"her company alone": McIlwaine, *The Minutes of the Council and General Court of Colonial Virginia 1622–1632, 1670–1676*, 41–42.

"Judgement . . . judgement": McIlwaine, *Council and General Court*, 42.

"I Grevell Pooley preacher": McIlwaine, *Council and General Court*, 42.

3: Goodwives to New England

"A woman has been": Moynihan, Russet, and Crumpacker, eds., *Second to None: A Documentary History of American Women*, 85.

"hideous and desolate wilderness": *A History of Plimoth Plantation* quoted in Pearce, ed., *Colonial American Writing*, 46.

"Some of the best things": Rae, ed., *Witnessing America: The Library of Congress Book of Firsthand Accounts of Life in America, 1600–1900*, 225.

"Being the depth of winter": *History of Plimoth Plantation*, quoted in Pearce, ed., *Colonial American Writing*, 48.

"The women now went willingly": Rae, *Witnessing America*, 134.

"mundayes and frydayes at 5": Rae, *Witnessing America*, 34.

"Those that scaped": Bradford, *History of Plymouth Plantation*, 579.
"wrought so wonderfully for them": Bradford, *History of Plymouth Plantation*, 579.
"severe and proud Dame": See the chapter on Mary Rowlandson for more of her observations on Weetamoo.
"The Indians who were prisoners": Berkin, *First Generations: Women in Colonial America*, 54.
"If she had an opportunity": Ulrich, *Good Wives: Image and Reality in the Lives of Women in Northern New England, 1650–1750*, 220.
"She caught hold on": Rae, *Witnessing America*, 254.
"While we were in this": Ulrich, *Good Wives*, 219.
"mixed assembly" and *"unwifed herself"*: Ulrich, *Good Wives*, 112.
"Families . . . are the first foundation": Moynihan, Russet, and Crumpacker, *Second to None*, 58.
"worketh willingly with": Proverbs 31:13 and 27.

Anne Hutchinson
Unless otherwise noted, all quotes from Anne Hutchinson's 1637 court trial sourced from America and the World, "Anne Hutchinson Trial Testimony, 1637," www.americaandtheworld.com/assets/media/pdfs/Hutchinson.pdf.
"Here is a great stir": LaPlante, *American Jezebel: The Uncommon Life of Anne Hutchinson, the Woman Who Defied the Puritans*, 53.
"God's dealing with her": LaPlante, *American Jezebel*, 115.
"so fierce" and *"the lions after"*: LaPlante, *American Jezebel*, 120.
"errors taken from": LaPlante, *American Jezebel*, 160.
"If this be error": LaPlante, *American Jezebel*, 173.
"did not hold diverse": LaPlante, *American Jezebel*, 174.
"She is of a most dangerous": LaPlante, *American Jezebel*, 181–2.
"For, you see, she is": LaPlante, *American Jezebel*, 186.
"how the dishonor you have brought": LaPlante, *American Jezebel*, 187.
"the uttermost to raze": LaPlante, *American Jezebel*, 188.
"And though I have not heard": LaPlante, *American Jezebel*, 188.
"I never held any": LaPlante, *American Jezebel*, 196.
"I do acknowledge I was": LaPlante, *American Jezebel*, 195.
"you have stepped out of": LaPlante, *American Jezebel*, 200.
"I look at her as a dangerous": LaPlante, *American Jezebel*, 201–202.

"In the name of our Lord": LaPlante, *American Jezebel*, 204.
"The Lord judges not": LaPlante, *American Jezebel*, 207.
"see how the wisdom": LaPlante, *American Jezebel*, 218.
"From the Church of Boston": LaPlante, *American Jezebel*, 221.
"I am more nearly tied": LaPlante, *American Jezebel*, 222.
"out this woeful woman": LaPlante, *American Jezebel*, 224.

Anne Dudley Bradstreet
"unbelief . . . whether it be a woman's": Introduction to *The Tenth Muse*.
All other quotes are taken from *The Complete Works of Anne Bradstreet*.

The Captivity of Mary Rowlandson
All quotes in this section come from Mary Rowlandson's *The Narrative of the Captivity and the Restoration of Mrs. Mary Rowlandson, 1682*, read at http://csivc.csi.cuny.edu/history/files/lavender/rownarr.html.

4: Weary, Weary, Weary, O

"Their servants they distinguish": The History and Present State of Virginia, quoted in Pearce, ed., *Colonial American Writing*, 502.
"as much love, respect": Moynihan, Russet, and Crumpacker, eds., *Second to None: A Documentary History of American Women*, 35.
"purged" and "foule": Moynihan, Russet, and Crumpacker, *Second to None*, 38.
"have the best luck here": Spruill, *Women's Life and Work in the Southern Colonies*, 137.
"If they be but civil": Spruill, *Women's Life and Work*, 15.
"rooting in the ground": Jones, *American Work: Four Centuries of Black and White Labor*, 23.
"the meanest Cottages": Spruill, *Women's Life and Work*, 20–21.
"to make a Cropp": Jones, *American Work*, 42.
"We and the Negroes": Jones, *American Work*, 76.
"too much worke": Jones, *American Work*, 56.
"beating at the mortar": Jones, *American Work*, 66.
"more and more troublesome": Jones, *American Work*, 56.
"as soft as a sponge": Moynihan, Russet, and Crumpacker, *Second to None*, 67.

"offended [him] in the highest": Letter of Elizabeth Sprigs to Mr. John Sprigs, Sept. 22, 1756.
"that some dissolute": Jones, *American Work*, 72.
"Maid servants of good honest stock": Jones, *American Work*, 48.
"both men and womenkind": Jones, *American Work*, 133.
"to the disgrace of our Nation": Kohlmetz, ed., *The Study of American History*, 57.
"doth not alter the condition": Kohlmetz, *Study of American History*, 57.
"If she had her just right": Kulikoff, *Tobacco and Slaves: The Development of the Southern Culture in the Chesapeake, 1680–1800*, 377.
"laboring in the Corn": Jones, *American Work*, 78.
"It is therefore advantageous": Purvis, *Almanacs of American Life: Colonial America to 1763*, 325.
"Sufficient Distinction is also made": Pearce, *Colonial American Writing*, 503.
"continual aspiring after their": Jones, *American Work*. 126.

Elizabeth Ashbridge
Unless otherwise noted, all quotes in this section taken from Elizabeth Ashbridge, *Some Account of the Fore Part of the Life of Elizabeth Ashbridge*, read at Early Americas Digital Archive, http://mith.umd.edu/eada/html/display.php?docs=ashbridge_account.xml&action=show.
"since my Absence was so": National Humanities Center, "Becoming American: The British Atlantic Colonies, 1660–1783."
"I was a Stranger": National Humanities Center, "Becoming American."
"a Difference that happened": National Humanities Center, "Becoming American."
"the Utmost Hardship": National Humanities Center, "Becoming American."
"the Town Whipper": National Humanities Center, "Becoming American."
"told it before his wife": National Humanities Center, "Becoming American."
"was not Sufficiently Punished": National Humanities Center, "Becoming American."

5: Up to Their Elbows in Housewifery

"tables fournished with porke": Spruill, *Women's Life and Work in the Southern Colonies*, 67.

She'd salted and smoked: Ulrich, *Good Wives: Image and Reality in the Lives of Women in Northern New England, 1650–1750*, 19–24.

"She may love and obey": Ulrich, *Good Wives*, 20.

For more on colonial medicine see the 1690s notebook of physician Thomas Palmer, *The Admirable Secrets of Physick and Chyrurgery*, ed. Thomas Rogers Forbes (New Haven, CT: Yale University Press), 1984.

"No sooner come, but gone": Bradstreet, *The Complete Works of Anne Bradstreet*, 188.

"They are everyday up to their Elbows": Spruill, *Women's Life and Work*, 64.

"sameness . . . throughout the year": Ulrich, *Good Wives*, 142.

"These poems are the fruit": Introduction to *The Tenth Muse*.

"her trouble and charge": Spruill, *Women's Life and Work*, 303.

"A Virginia Negro woman": Spruill, *Women's Life and Work*, 95.

"I meddle not": Ulrich, *Good Wives*, 46.

"where the best attendance": Spruill, *Women's Life and Work*, 272.

"the said Mistress Brent": Moynihan, Russet, and Crumpacker, eds., *Second to None: A Documentary History of American Women*, 81.

"We do Verily believe": Carr, "Margaret Brent (ca. 1601–1671)," Maryland.gov.

"will be kindly pleased": Moynihan, Russet, and Crumpacker, *Second to None*, 115.

"We are House Keepers": Moynihan, Russet, and Crumpacker, *Second to None*, 121.

"All persons indebted to her": Spruill, *Women's Life and Work*, 285.

"into a sad infirmity": Koehler, "The Case of the American Jezebels: Anne Hutchinson and Female Agitation During the Years of Antinomian Turmoil, 1636–1640," 58.

Margaret Hardenbroeck Philipse

"free agent of New Amsterdam": Zimmerman, *The Women of the House: How a Colonial She-Merchant Built a Mansion, a Fortune, and a Dynasty*, 15.

"Your sacred Majesty": Zimmerman, Women of the House, 109.
1,713 beaver pelts: Zimmerman, Women of the House, 113.
"You have the devil in you!": Zimmerman, Women of the House, 121.
"miserable covetous": Zimmerman, Women of the House, 121.

The Journey of Sarah Kemble Knight
All quotes in this section from Sarah Knight, The Journal of Madam
   Knight, electronic edition from Early Americas Digital Archive,
   http://mith.umd.edu/eada/html/display.php?docs=knight
   _journal.xml&action=show.
"taxed twenty shillings": Caulkins, History of New London, Connecticut,
   372.

6: Daughters of Eve
"Read often the Matrimonial Service": Spruill, Women's Life and Work in
   the Southern Colonies, 164.
"No obey": Morgan, Virginians at Home: Family Life in the Eighteenth Century, 47–8.
"the very being or legal": Ulrich, Good Wives: Image and Reality in the Lives
   of Women in Northern New England, 1650–1750, 7.
"gracyously placed thy good": Ulrich, Good Wives, 6.
"The woman's own choice": Miller, The First Frontier: Life in Colonial
   America, 204
"a special Care and Tenderness": Moynihan, Russet, and Crumpacker,
   eds., Second to None: A Documentary History of American Women, 59.
"Mrs. Mechison tells me": Ulrich, Good Wives, 109.
"the larger share of Reason": Moynihan, Russet, and Crumpacker, Second to None, 128.
"wanteth" a woman's "Gentleness": Moynihan, Russet, and Crumpacker, Second to None, 129.
"A woman who breaks her marriage vows": Spruill, Women's Life and
   Work, 173.
"If my daughter likes him": Morgan, Virginians at Home, 34.
"endowed with all agreeable": Spruill, Women's Life and Work, 154.
"Strict Vertue": Ulrich, Good Wives, 84–5.
"To whom will you fly": Pollock, A Lasting Relationship: Parents and Children over Three Centuries, 271–2.

"one of the most antick": Morgan, *Virginians at Home*, 47.

"The various & excellent Endowments": From the author's notes taken at Evelyn's tomb.

"against her duty": Pollock, *Lasting Relationship*, 274.

"They that marry": Ulrich, *Good Wives*, 121.

"A virtuous woman should reject": Spruill, *Women's Life and Work*, 149.

"reckoned a stale maid": Spruill, *Women's Life and Work*, 139.

"An old maid is one": Spruill, *Women's Life and Work*, 138.

"The Sin of my Mother": Moynihan, Russet, and Crumpacker, *Second to None*, 126.

"How soon, my Dear": Pearce, *Colonial American Writing*, 407.

"Died in Child Birth": Spruill, *Women's Life and Work*, 52.

Society viewed mothers: Ulrich, *Good Wives*, 154.

"Look to my little Babes": Pearce, *Colonial American Writing*, 407.

"no vile names or": Bryan, *Martha Washington: First Lady of Liberty*, 43. Martha Washington's first husband was Daniel Parke Custis, son of the unhappy Frances Parke and John Custis.

In 1744 Susannah Cooper: Spruill, *Women's Life and Work*, 348.

"Poor dear babe": Spruill, *Women's Life and Work*, 171.

"in a very imprudent manner": Spruill, *Women's Life and Work*, 178.

"John Cantwell has the impudence": Spruill, *Women's Life and Work*, 181.

"My wife Alice": Berkin, *First Generations: Women in Colonial America*, 17.

"She hath at all times": Spruill, *Women's Life and Work*, 165.

"I do think it my Duty": Spruill, *Women's Life and Work*, 165.

"Brabling women": Spruill, *Women's Life and Work*, 331.

"pleading their bellies": Spruill, *Women's Life and Work*, 326.

"black Indians": Norton, *In the Devil's Snare: The Salem Witchcraft Crisis of 1692*, 59.

"I am an innocent person": From the records of the Court of Oyer and Terminer, 1692, property of the Supreme Judicial Court, Division of Archives and Records Preservation on deposit at the Peabody Essex Museum, Salem, Massachusetts.

"We ourselves were not capable": Norton, *Devil's Snare*, 312.

Martha Corey

"Comitted sundry acts of Witchcraft": Arrest warrant of Martha Corey, from the records of the Court of Oyer and Terminer, 1692,

property of the Supreme Judicial Court, Division of Archives and
Records Preservation on deposit at the Peabody Essex Museum,
Salem, Massachusetts.

Unless otherwise noted, all other quotes are from the arrest warrant,
depositions, examination, and indictment of Martha Corey from
the records of the Court of Oyer and Terminer, 1692, property
of the Supreme Judicial Court, Division of Archives and Records
Preservation on deposit at the Peabody Essex Museum, Salem,
Massachusetts. Modern punctuation has been added in a few
places to make the meaning clearer.

"and Goodey Corey you be a turnning": Norton, *In the Devil's Snare: The
Salem Witchcraft Crisis of 1692*, 48.

"goodey Cory to be gone": Norton, *Devil's Snare*, 48.

"It was observed several times": Lawson, *A Brief and True Narrative of
Some Remarkable passages Relating to Sundry Persons Afflicted by
Witchcraft at Salem Village (1692)*, cited in "The Salem Witch Trials,
1692," EyeWitness to History.com

"grievous torment in her bowels": Lawson, *Brief and True Narrative*.

"and hit Goodwife Corey": Lawson, *Brief and True Narrative*.

In April, Martha's accusers sent Giles to prison, too, accusing him
of witchcraft. Giles Corey pleaded not guilty, refused a trial, and
maintained his silence. The court tried to force a confession,
crushing him beneath stones. Giles Corey died around September
18, 1692.

"the Devil hindered it": Norton, *Devil's Snare*, 278.

"an Eminent Prayer upon the Ladder": Norton, *Devil's Snare*, 278.

7: A Changing World

"I wrote my father": Pinckney, *The Letterbook of Eliza Lucas Pinckney,
1739–1762*, 8.

"We are 17 miles by land": Pinckney, *Letterbook of Eliza*, 7.

"She is a very civil": Spruill, *Women's Life and Work in the Southern Colonies*, 81.

"I lay down before the fire": Miller, *The First Frontier: Life in Colonial
America*, 137.

"With them [the Seneca]": Axtell, ed., *The Indian Peoples of Eastern America: A Documentary History of the Sexes*, 138.

"killed or carried away": Ulrich, *Good Wives: Image and Reality in the Lives of Women in Northern New England, 1650–1750*, 167.

"The English have taken away": Axtell, *Beyond 1492: Encounters in Colonial North America*, 150.

"The English have no sense": Axtell, *Beyond 1492*, 132.

"Moreover," remarked Carolina trader: Moynihan, Russet, and Crumpacker, eds., *Second to None: A Documentary History of American Women*, 39.

"There now remain": Purvis, *Almanacs of American Life: Colonial America to 1763*, 35.

Immigrants arrived regularly: Purvis, *Almanacs of American Life*, 129.

"so much does Their Taste": Spruill, *Women's Life and Work*, 131.

"Thigh that Woodcock": Spruill, *Women's Life and Work*, 70.

"I have been thinking": Ulrich, *Good Wives*, 68.

"77 Pounds of butter": Ulrich, *Good Wives*, 71.

In one year, Mrs. Carter: Spruill, *Women's Life and Work*, 66.

Some slaves ran: Kulikoff, *Tobacco and Slaves: The Development of the Southern Culture in the Chesapeake, 1680–1800*, 378.

"in some Negro Quarter": Kulikoff, *Tobacco and Slaves*, 373.

"My wife," wrote Byrd: Morgan, *Virginians at Home: Family Life in the Eighteenth Century*, 59.

"soundly whipped": Miller, *First Frontier*, 151.

"by being the First of them": Ulrich, *Good Wives*, 153.

"heav'nly fair": Ulrich, *Good Wives*, 114.

"Consider the fearful danger": Kohlmetz, ed., *The Study of American History*, 136.

"their first permanent attention": Moynihan, Russet, and Crumpacker, *Second to None*, 144.

Boston boasted 13,000 citizens: Purvis, *Almanacs of American Life*, 222, 226, 228, 224.

"An universal Mirth and Glee": Spruill, *Women's Life and Work*, 90.

"encourage Industry and": Jones, *American Work: Four Centuries of Black and White Labor*, 159.

Eliza Lucas Pinckney

All quotes in this section are from *The Letterbook of Eliza Lucas Pinckney, 1739–1762*.

Eve, and Others, Belonging to the Randolphs
"Little Aggy & her children": Last Will and Testament of Peyton Randolph.
"are able and willing": Lord Dunmore's Proclamation, read online at Library of Congress.
"the aged, the infirm": Rhodehamel, *The American Revolution: Writings from the War of Independence,* 85.
"I give to my Nephew": Last Will and Testament of Betty Randolph.
"and that of these about 27,000": Raphael, *A People's History of the American Revolution: How Common People Shaped the Fight for Independence,* 296.
"Twenty Dollars Reward": Virginia Gazette or American Advertiser, February 2, 1782.
"Whereas Eve's bad behavior": Last Will and Testament of Betty Randolph.

Christiana Campbell & Jane Vobe
"I Beg Leave": Virginia Gazette, October 1, 1771.
"February 6, 1772": Virginia Gazette.
"There is not a publick house": Colonial Williamsburg Foundation Library Research Report Series-1102.
"Mr. Pratt, a portrait painter": Virginia Gazette, March 4, 1773.
"Lost in the Garden": Virginia Gazette, May 20, 1773.
"a little old Woman": Colonial Williamsburg Foundation Library Research Report Series-1102.

8: A Tapestry of Lives

"I have had a Smart Combat": Moynihan, Russet, and Crumpacker, eds., *Second to None: A Documentary History of American Women,* 140.
"My whole Prospects in this world": Moynihan, Russet, and Crumpacker, *Second to None,* 141.
"the better strengthening": Kohlmetz, ed., *The Study of American History,* 133.

BIBLIOGRAPHY

Books and Articles

Ashbridge, Elizabeth. *Some Account of the Fore Part of the Life of Elizabeth Ashbridge*. Electronic edition available from Early Americas Digital Archive. http://mith.umd.edu/eada/html/display.php ?docs=ashbridge_account.xml&action=show, and http://national humanitiescenter.org/pds/becomingamer/growth/text5/ash bridge.pdf.

Axtell, James. *Beyond 1492: Encounters in Colonial North America*. New York: Oxford University Press, 1992.

Axtell, James, ed. *The Indian Peoples of Eastern America: A Documentary History of the Sexes*. New York: Oxford University Press, 1981.

Berkin, Carol. *First Generations: Women in Colonial America*. New York: Hill & Wang, 1996.

Billings, Warren M. *Jamestown and the Founding of the Nation*. Gettysburg, PA: Thomas Publications for the National Park Service, 1991.

Bradford, William. *History of Plymouth Plantation*. Electronic edition available from Early Americas Digital Archive. www.mith.umd .edu/eada/html/display.php?docs=bradford_history.xml.

Bradstreet, Anne. *The Complete Works of Anne Bradstreet.* Edited by Joseph McElrath Jr. and Allan Robb. Woodbridge, CT: Twayne, 1981.

Bryan, Helen. *Martha Washington: First Lady of Liberty.* New York: John Wiley & Sons, 2002.

Caulkins, Frances Manwaring. *History of New London, Connecticut: From the First Survey of the Coast in 1612 to 1852.* New London, 1852.

Carr, Lois G., and Lorena Walsh. "The Planter's Wife: The Experience of White Women in Seventeenth-Century Maryland." *William & Mary Quarterly,* 3rd ser., 34, no. 4 (October 1977): 542–571.

David, Richard, ed. *Hakluyt's Voyages.* Boston: Houghton Mifflin, 1981.

Demos, John. *The Tried and the True: Native American Women Confronting Colonization.* New York: Oxford University Press, 1995.

Jones, Jacqueline. *American Work: Four Centuries of Black and White Labor.* New York: W. W. Norton, 1998.

Kamensky, Jane. *The Colonial Mosaic: American Women, 1600–1760.* New York: Oxford University Press, 1995.

Kingsbury, Susan Myra, ed. *The Records of the Virginia Company of London.* Vol 4. Washington, DC: Government Printing Office, 1906. https://openlibrary.org/books/OL7107468M/The_records_of_the_Virginia_Company_of_London.

Knight, Sarah. *The Journal of Madam Knight.* Electronic edition available from Early Americas Digital Archive. http://mith.umd.edu/eada/html/display.php?docs=knight_journal.xml&action=show.

Koehler, Lyle. "The Case of American Jezebels: Anne Hutchinson and Female Agitation During the Years of Antinomian Turmoil, 1636–1640." *William & Mary Quarterly,* 3rd ser., 31, no. 1 (January 1974): 55–78.

Kohlmetz, Ernest, ed. *The Study of American History.* Vol. 1. Connecticut: Dushkin, 1973.

Kulikoff, Allan. *Tobacco and Slaves: The Development of Southern Cultures in the Chesapeake, 1680–1800.* Chapel Hill: University of North Carolina Press, 1986.

Kupperman, Karen. "Fear of Hot Climates in the Anglo-American Experience." *William & Mary Quarterly,* 3rd ser., 41 (April 1984): 24–40.

LaPlante, Eve. *American Jezebel: The Uncommon Life of Anne Hutchinson, the Woman Who Defied the Puritans.* New York: Harper Collins, 2005.

Lawson, Deodat. *A Brief and True Narrative of Some Remarkable passages Relating to Sundry Persons Afflicted by Witchcraft at Salem Village (1692),* cited in "The Salem Witch Trials, 1692." EyeWitness to History.com. www.eyewitnesstohistory.com/salem.htm.

McIlwaine, H. R., ed. *The Minutes of the Council and General Court of Colonial Virginia 1622–1632, 1670–1676.* Richmond, VA: Colonial Press, Everett Waddey Co., 1924. https://archive.org/details/minutesofcouncil00virg.

Miller, John C. *The First Frontier: Life in Colonial America.* Lanham, MD: University Press of America, 1986.

Moynihan, Ruth B., Cynthia Russett, and Laurie Crumpacker, eds. *Second to None: A Documentary History of American Women.* Vol. 1, *From the Sixteenth Century to 1865.* Lincoln: University of Nebraska Press, 1993.

Morgan, Edmund. *Virginians at Home: Family Life in the Eighteenth Century.* Williamsburg, VA: Colonial Williamsburg Foundation, 1952.

Norton, Mary Beth. *In the Devil's Snare: The Salem Witchcraft Crisis of 1692.* New York: Alfred A. Knopf, 2002.

Palmer, Thomas. *The Admirable Secrets of Physick and Chyrurgery.* Edited by Thomas Rogers Forbes. New Haven: Yale University Press, 1984.

Pearce, Roy H., ed. *Colonial American Writing.* New York: Holt, Rinehart and Winston, 1969.

Pinckney, Eliza Lucas. *The Letterbook of Eliza Lucas Pinckney, 1739–1762.* Edited by Elise Pinckney. Columbia: University of South Carolina Press, 1997.

Pollock, Linda. *A Lasting Relationship: Parents and Children over Three Centuries.* Hanover, MA: University Press of New England, 1987.

Purchas, Samuel. *Purchas His Pilgrimage.* Electronic edition available from Open Library. https://openlibrary.org/books/OL22890960M/Purchas_his_pilgrimage.

Purvis, Thomas L. *Almanacs of American Life: Colonial America to 1763.* New York: Fact on File, 1999.

Rae, Noel, ed. *Witnessing America: The Library of Congress Book of First-hand Accounts of Life in America, 1600–1900*. New York: Stonesong, 1996.

Ransome, David. "Wives for Virginia, 1621." *William & Mary Quarterly*, 3rd ser., 48, no. 1 (January 1991): 3–18.

Raphael, Ray. *A People's History of the American Revolution: How Common People Shaped the Fight for Independence*. New York: New Press, 2001.

Rhodehamel, John, ed. *The American Revolution: Writings from the War of Independence*. New York: Library of America, 2001.

Rountree, Helen. *Pocahontas, Powhatan, Opechancanough: Three Indian Lives Changed by Jamestown*. Charlottesville: University of Virginia Press, 2005.

Rowlandson, Mary. *The Narrative of the Captivity and the Restoration of Mrs. Mary Rowlandson, 1682*. Electronic edition available at http://csivc.csi.cuny.edu/history/files/lavender/rownarr.html.

Schlesinger, Catherine S. *Christiana Campbell's Tavern Architectural Report*. Colonial Williamsburg Foundation Library Research Report Series: 1102. Williamsburg, VA: Colonial Williamsburg Foundation Library, 1990.

Smith, John. *The Generall Historie of Virginia, New England, and the Summer Isles, 1624*. Electronic edition available from Documenting the American South. www.docsouth.unc.edu/southlit/smith/smith.html.

Smith, John. *Travels and Works of Captain John Smith: President of Virginia and Admiral of New England, 1580–1631*. Edited by Edward Arber. 2 vols. Edinburgh: John Grant, 1910.

Smith, John. *A True Relation of Occurences and Accidents in Virginia, 1608*. Electronic edition available from Early Americas Digital Archive. http://mith.umd.edu/eada/html/display.php?docs=smith_true relation.xml&action=show.

Spruill, Julia C. *Women's Life and Work in the Southern Colonies*. New York: W. W. Norton, 1972. Originally published in 1938 by University of North Carolina Press.

Strachey, William. *The Historie of Travaile into Virginia Britannia, 1612*. London, 1849.

Townsend, Camilla. *Pocahontas and the Powhatan Dilemma*. New York: Hill and Wang, 2004.

Ulrich, Laurel. *Good Wives: Image and Reality in the Lives of Women in Northern New England, 1650–1750*. New York: Alfred A. Knopf, 1982.

Wright, Louis B. *The Cultural Life of the American Colonies*. New York: Harper and Brothers, 1957.

Zimmerman, Jean. *The Women of the House: How a Colonial She-Merchant Built a Mansion, a Fortune, and a Dynasty*. New York: Harcourt, 2006.

Online Sources

Carr, Lois Green. "Margaret Brent (ca. 1601–1671)." Archives of Maryland. http://msa.maryland.gov/megafile/msa/speccol/sc3500/sc3520/002100/002177/html/bio.html.

Colonial Williamsburg Foundation website:
Last Will and Testament of Betty Randolph. www.history.org/almanack/people/bios/bioran.cfm.
Last Will and Testament of Peyton Randolph. www.history.org/Almanack/people/bios/bioran.cfm.
"VirginiaGazettes." http://research.history.org/DigitalLibrary/va-gazettes/.

The records of Martha Corey's examination, her arrest warrant, and depositions against her appear in the records of the Court of Oyer and Terminer, 1692, property of the Supreme Judicial Court, Division of Archives and Records Preservation on deposit at the Peabody Essex Museum, Salem, Massachusetts. http://salem.lib.virginia.edu/people?group.num=G07&mbio.num=mb33.

Hutchinson, Anne. Trial testimony, 1637. www.swarthmore.edu/SocSci/bdorsey1/41docs/30-hut.html.

National Humanities Center. "Becoming American: The British Atlantic Colonies, 1690–1763." Toolbox Library: Primary Resources in U.S. History & Literature. http://nationalhumanitiescenter.org/pds/becomingamer/indes.htm.

Randolph, Harrison. Eve's runaway ad in the *Virginia Gazette*. www2.vcdh.virginia.edu/gos/search/relatedAd.php?adFile=vg1782.xml&adId=v1782020017.

Reutiman, Joe. "The Forgotten Kidnapping: The Transformation of the Pocahontas Captivity Story." The Pocahontas Archive. http://digital.lib.lehigh.edu/trial/pocahontas/essays.php?id=8.

Rolfe, John. Letter to Governor Dale. Virtual Jamestown. www.virtualjamestown.org/rolfe_letter.html.

Sprigs, Elizabeth. Letter to Mr. John Sprigs, September 22, 1756. http://historymatters.gmu.edu/d/5796.

Woodbridge, John. Introduction to The Tenth Muse. http://college.cengage.com/english/lauter/heath/4e/students/author_pages/colonial/bradstreet_an.html.

INDEX

towns, advantages of living in, 177–178

uprisings, 97

usus, 124

Uttamatomakin, 31, 33

Van de Passe, Simon, 34

Vaughan, William, 12

villages, advantages of living in, 177–178

Virginia, 11–20, 88, 95, 171

Virginia Assembly, 40, 93

Virginia Company, 14, 32, 34

Virginia General Assembly, 197

Virginia House of Burgess, 150

Vobe, Jane, 197–199, 201, 202

Wahunsonacock. *See* Powhatan

Walcott, Mary, 155, 160, 161, 165

Wampanoag, 4, 44, 48, 75

Wamsutta, 48

Wappoo (farm), 179, 181, 183

Washington, George, 151, 168, 187, 199, 200

weddings, 144

Weetamoo, 48–49, 81–82

Weld, Thomas, 60, 65

werowance, 22, 23

Werowocomoco, 22, 25

West Indies, 47, 93

Wetherburn's Tavern, 201

Wheelwright, John, 55

Whitaker, Alexander, 28

White, Susannah, 43, 45

Whitefield, George, 176

widows, 7–8, 116, 120–121, 124, 151, 178

Willard, Samuel, 52, 139

Williams, Abigail, 153–154, 161, 162, 165

Williams, Roger, 4, 8, 9, 16

Williamsburg, Virginia, 198–199

Wilson, John, 64

Winthrop, John, 46, 50

Anne Hutchinson and, 43, 53, 55–59, 61, 64–65

on education of women, 121

on marriage, 138–139

Winthrop, Margaret, 46

witch hunts, 152–156

Wittimore. *See* Weetamoo

wives

daily chores of, 108–115

Dutch law and, 124

expectations of, 138, 149, 171–174, 203

recruitment of, 14, 87–88, 117–118

women

colonial view of, 52, 137–139

religion and, 176

single. *see* spinsters

Wood, William, 87

Woodbridge, John, 67

Yapassus, 27, 28

Zeisberger, David, 3, 6